Last Rites

BOOKS BY JOHN LUKACS

The Great Powers and Eastern Europe

Tocqueville: The European Revolution
and Correspondence with Gobineau (editor)

A History of the Cold War

Decline and Rise of Europe

A New History of the Cold War

Historical Consciousness; or, The Remembered Past

The Passing of the Modern Age

A Sketch of the History of Chestnut Hill College, 1924–1974

The Last European War: September 1939–December 1941

1945: Year Zero

Philadelphia, Patricians and Philistines, 1900–1950

Outgrowing Democracy: A History of the
United States in the Twentieth Century

Budapest 1900: A Historical Portrait of a
City and Its Culture

Confessions of an Original Sinner

The Duel: The Eighty-Day Struggle Between Churchill and Hitler

The End of the Twentieth Century and the End of the Modern Age

Destinations Past: Traveling through History with John Lukacs

George F. Kennan and the Origins of Containment,
1944–1946: The Kennan-Lukacs Correspondence

The Hitler of History

A Thread of Years

Five Days in London: May 1940

A Student's Guide to the Study of History

At the End of an Age

Churchill: Visionary. Statesman. Historian.

A New Republic: A History of the United States in the Twentieth Century

Democracy and Populism: Fear and Hatred

Remembered Past: John Lukacs on History,
Historians, and Historical Knowledge

June 1941: Hitler and Stalin

George Kennan: A Study of Character

Blood, Toil, Tears, and Sweat: The Dire Warning,
Churchill's First Speech as Prime Minister

Last Rites

John Lukacs

YALE UNIVERSITY PRESS   NEW HAVEN & LONDON

Set in Janson type by Integrated Publishing Solutions, Grand Rapids, Michigan.
Printed in the United States of America by
Thomson-Shore, Inc., Dexter, Michigan.

ISBN 978-0-300-11438-6 (cloth : alk. paper)
Library of Congress Control Number: 2008930380

A catalogue record for this book is available from the British Library.

This paper meets the requirements of ANSI/NISO Z39.48-1992
(Permanence of Paper).
It contains 30 percent postconsumer waste (PCW) and is certified by the
Forest Stewardship Council (FSC).

10 9 8 7 6 5 4 3 2 1

For Father Francis X. Meehan,
non genitor sed pastor

Contents

Last Rites

A Bad Fifteen Minutes

About twenty years ago, at the age of sixty-five, I wrote a kind of autobiography, entitled *Confessions of an Original Sinner* (published in 1990). It was fairly well received, and here and there is still in print. It was an auto-history rather than a routine autobiography. (I started it with two sentences: "This is not a history of my life. It is a history of my thoughts and beliefs.") In one of its chapters, entitled "Writing," I wrote about what and why I kept writing, and about some of the books I had written during the then forty years of my career as a historian. Well, now, during the following twenty, I wrote more books (though probably with fewer pages) than in the preceding forty, for all kinds of reasons. But in this there must be no place for a chortling summary listing (or even a melancholy one) of my published achievements. So my plan of this book is the reverse of *Confessions*, which proceeded, say, from 1924 to 1987, through the first sixty years of my life and from the personal to something impersonal, from something like an autobiography to something like a personal philosophy. Now my sequence will be that of a summing up of my recognitions of *our* present knowledge of the world to memories of *my* private life, from something like a philosophy to something like an autobiography. The precedence of the former: because of my conviction of its importance. That is my obsessive insistence that human knowledge is neither objective nor subjective but personal and participant—while (among other things) that we, and our earth, are at the center of the universe.

First things first is not always, and not necessarily, the best way to begin a book. I am taking a risk: but then all art, including writing, must contain a risk. Besides—I do not know who the readers of this book will be. And I know that because of the circumstances and the conditions of the world we now live in, their attention spans (very much including those of academics, intellectuals, philosophers, scholars, yes, myself too) have become, even if not altogether "brutish" and "nasty"—narrowed, constricted, and *short*. So, readers: please bear with me for fifteen minutes or so.

"Un mauvais quart d'heure," the French say, of those painful fifteen minutes when a son must tell his father that he failed in school; or that he stole; or when a man thinks he now must tell his woman that he will leave her.* They have to tell the truth: *a* truth.

First things first. This is the most important part of this book. For fifteen minutes bear with me.

∎

Un mauvais quart d'heure. Telling a truth.

Step by step.

Or: "*Architecture of a new humanism.*"

Oh, I was still very young when I *saw* that historians, or indeed scholars and scientists and human beings of all kinds, are *not* objective. And then, the trouble was with many who thought and wished to impress the world that they *were* objective. There are still many historians and even more scientists of that kind, men with gray ice on their faces.

But isn't Objectivity an ideal? No: because the purpose of human knowledge—indeed, of human life itself—is not accuracy, and not even certainty; it is understanding.

An illustration. To attempt to be "objective" about Hitler or Stalin is one thing; to attempt to understand them is another; and the second is not inferior to the first. Can we expect a victim to be "objective" about someone who did him harm? Can we ex-

---

*Ah! But in 2009, at the end of an entire civilization, do we still live in a world where there still are, where there still must be, mauvais quarts d'heure?

pect a Jewish man to be "objective" about Hitler? Perhaps not. Yet we *may* expect him, or indeed anyone, to attempt to understand. But that attempt must depend on the *how*, on the very quality of his participation, on the approach of his own mind, including at least a modicum of understanding his own self. After all, Hitler and Stalin were human beings, so they were not *entirely* or *essentially* different from any other person now thinking about them.

History involves the knowledge of human beings of other human beings. And this knowledge is different from other kinds of knowledge, since human beings are the most complex organisms in the entire universe.

The ideal of objectivity is the total, the antiseptic separation of the knower from the known. Understanding involves an approach, that of getting closer. In any event, and about everything: there is, there can be, no essential separation of the knower from the known.

But: are there no objective facts? Ah! Beside the limits of "objectivity" there are the limits of "facts."

Yes, there are "facts." The door was open. The water was at a boil. The house was on fire. Napoleon lost at Waterloo. But "facts" have at least three limits—perhaps especially for historians. One: for us the meaning of every "fact" exists only through our instant association and comparison of it with other facts. Two: for us the meaning of every fact depends on its statement, on the words with which it is expressed. Three: for us these words depend on their purposes. (There are statements in which every "fact" may be correct, and yet the meaning, tendency, purpose of their statements may be wrong.)

We are human beings, with our inevitable limitations. We think in words. Especially when it comes to history, which has no language of its own, no scientific terminology: we speak and write and teach it in words. Besides, words and language have their own histories. One pertinent example: four or five hundred years ago the very words *objective, subjective, fact* meant not what they now mean or pretend to mean. Words are not finite categories but meanings—what they mean for us, to us. They have their own histories and lives and deaths, their magical powers and their limits.

■

Historical knowledge—indeed, any kind of human knowledge—is necessarily subjective. That is what I tended to think in my early twenties. Soon I found that I was necessarily wrong: that subjectivity is merely the other, the obverse side of objectivism and objectivity, that there is something wrong with the entire Cartesian coin, of a world divided into Object and Subject: because Subjectivism as much as Objectivism is *determinist*.

Yes, every human being sees the world in his own way. That is inevitable: but not determined. We choose not only what and how we think but what and how we see. According to subjectivism *I* can think and see in only one (my) way; *he* in (his) another. This is wrong, because thinking and seeing are creative acts, coming from the inside, not the outside. Which is why we are responsible not only for how and what we do or say but for how and what we think and see. (Or: for what we want to think and for what we want to see.)

Very few people have recognized that the essence of National Socialism, including its biological racism, was something like subjectivist determinism, or call it idealistic determinism, or call it subjectivist idealism. The Jews are a spiritual, even more than a biological, race, Hitler once said. They think in a certain— their—way: they cannot think otherwise. A great historian, Johan Huizinga, saw something of this peril early. Around 1933—not referring to Germany or to Hitler—he wrote that "subjectivism" was a great danger. (The other great danger, for him, was the increasing domination of technology.)

There were a few historians who realized the limitations, indeed, the very ideal of Scientific Objectivity, at least in their profession. (One of them was Charles A. Beard, who slid into Subjectivism from Objectivism around that very time: but, unlike Huizinga, he could not see further.) Twenty-five or thirty years later it took Edward Hallett Carr, a former Marxist, to make the academy of professional historians hear what they, probably, were getting inclined to hear. (This is how and why the history of ideas is almost always woefully incomplete: not *what* but *when* it is that people are finally willing to hear something.) In *What Is History*, still a celebrated book, published in 1961, Carr declared: "Before you study the history, study the historian." Well, yes (though the reverse of that applies too: before you study the historian, study his history).* But Carr's thesis is nothing but Subjectivist Determinism: in his view a historian's background, and especially his social background, virtually determines the history he will write. This is nonsense: consider the sons of rich bourgeois who chose to become Marxists, or the offspring of Marxists who chose to become neoconservatives. The crucial word is: they *chose*.†

Besides—or perhaps more than "besides"—the subjectivist Carr could not really detach himself from the Cartesian, the Objective-Subjective terminology: "It does not follow that, because a mountain appears to take on different angles of vision, it has objectively no shape at all or an infinity of shapes." But the more "objective" our concept of the mountain, the more abstract that mountain becomes.‡

---

*That in reality, calls for more honesty, for a greater strength of mind. How often will historians dismiss a book because of its author, whom they do not like!

†To dabblers in the history of ideas it may be interesting that Carr's book nearly coincided with Thomas Kuhn's *The Structure of Scientific Revolutions* (1962), a much celebrated but an essentially useless and worthless book in which vocabulary substitutes for thought, and which slides close to Subjectivism, though it does not quite dare to espouse it, suggesting but unready to state that Science is but the result of scientists (that, à la Carr, "before you study the science, study the scientist").

‡Perspective is a component of reality. So is history: because history had to pass until men began to call and see it a *mountain*, that is, something different from hills or from other outcroppings.

7

A few years after Carr the old bourgeois ideal of Objectivism was falling apart. Postmodernism appeared, even though that term and the "postmodern" adjective were confusing. (Was the ideal of Objectivity just another bourgeois ideal, a "modern" one?) "Structuralism" and its proponents, many of them French, appeared; entire academic departments of literature took them seriously, even though they were hardly more than yet another academic fad. Their essence was, and remains, not much more than Subjectivism. They will not endure. What will, what must endure is the piecemeal recognition that the division of the world into objects and subjects belongs to history, as does every other human creation: that whatever realities Objectivity and its practical applications contained and may still contain, they are not perennial, not always and not forever valid.

■

Knowledge, neither "objective" nor "subjective," is always personal. Not individual: personal. The concept of the "individual" has been one of the essential misconceptions of political liberalism. Every human being is unique: but he does not exist alone. Not only is he dependent on others (a human baby for much longer than the offspring of other animals), his existence is inseparable from his relations with other human beings.

Every person has four relationships: with God, with himself, with other human beings, and with other living beings. The last two we can see and judge; the first two we may but surmise. But connected they are: we know some things about others through knowing some things about ourselves. That much is—or at least should be—obvious.

But there is more to that. Our knowledge is not only personal. It is participant. There is not—there cannot be—a separation of the knower from the known. And we must see farther than this. It is not enough to recognize the impossibility (perhaps even the absurdity) of the ideal of their antiseptic, "objective" separation. What concerns—or what should concern—us is something more than the inseparability, it is the *involvement* of the knower with the known. That this is so when it comes to the reading and the researching and the writing and the thinking of history should be rather obvious. "Detachment" from one's passions and memories is often commendable. But detachment, too, is something different from "separation"; it involves the ability (issuing from one's willingness) to achieve a stance of a longer or higher perspective: and the choice for such a stance does not necessarily mean a reduction of one's personal interest, of participation—perhaps even the contrary.

Interest includes, it involves participation. But keep in mind: participation is not, it cannot be complete. What "A" says to "B" is never *exactly* what "B" hears—usually because of his or her instant associations with some things other than the words of "A." Yes: their communications, *all* human communications, are necessarily incomplete—because of the complexity and the limitations of the human mind. But there is a wondrous compensation for this. That is that the charm of human communications resides precisely in their incompleteness, in the condition that what "B" hears is *not exactly* what "A" says—whence, in some instances, even the attraction of "A."*

But this inevitable involvement of the knower with the known does not exist only in the relations of human beings with other human beings. It involves, too, what we call "science," man's knowledge of physical things, of nature, of matter. I shall come to this too—soon. Before that, a mere few words about the relationship of mind and matter. Did—does—matter exist independent, without, the human mind? It did and it does: but without the human mind, its existence is meaningless—indeed, without

---

*Another obvious illustration of this condition is this. When we know a foreign (that is: another) language well, there is a charm in knowing (or, rather, understanding) that the very same words, with their very same origins, in the two languages may mean something slightly different. (Example: the English *honor* and the French *honneur*.)

Yet another condition, illustrating the impossibility of dividing Object from Subject. Consider what happens when we are concerned, anxious about someone who is dear to us. Can we separate our concerns for her from how that concern affects (and will affect) us? There *may* be an imbalance of these two concerns, between our thinking *mostly* about her and our thinking *mostly* about how her state affects or will affect us. But *in either case* these concerns are inseparable: both "objectivity" (an exclusive concentration on her condition) and "subjectivity" (an exclusive concentration on my condition) are impossible. Our consciousness and our knowledge, our concern and our expectations are participant and thus inseparable.

the human mind we cannot think of its "existence" at all. In this sense it may even be argued that Mind preceded and may precede Matter (or: what we see and then call matter).

■

In any case, or event, the relations of "mind" and "matter" are not simple. In any case or event* they are *not* mechanical.

What happens is what people think happens. At the time of its happening—and at least for some time thereafter. History is formed thereby.

What happens and what people think happens are inseparable. That human condition is inevitable. (Does pain exist without one's recognition of pain? When someone thinks he is unhappy he *is* unhappy. Etc.) What we think happens or happened may of course be wrong, something that we *may* recognize later, at another time. (Or not. Even then we may be right or wrong, since memory is not mechanical either but another creative function: we may clarify or deceive our memories too.)

This does not now matter. What matters is the necessary and historic recognition that the human mind intrudes into causality, into the relation of causes and effects.

Causality—the how? and why?—has varied forms and mean-

Event, not *fact*. Consider but the sound and meaning of *event*, as it flows from past to present, while *fact* gives the impression of something definite and done, fixed in the past.

ings (Aristotle and Saint Thomas Aquinas listed four): but for centuries the terms of mechanical causality have dominated our world and our categories of thinking. All of the practical applications of "science," everything that is technical, inevitably depend on mechanical causality, on its three conditions: (1) the same causes must have the same effects; (2) there must be an equivalence of causes and effects; (3) the causes must precede their effects. None of this necessarily applies to human beings, to the functioning of their minds, to their lives, and especially to their history.

Illustrations thereof. (1) Steam rising in a kettle: at a certain point, at a measurable temperature, the pressure becomes intolerable, an explosion is inevitable and determined: the lid of the kettle will fly off. But in human life the lid is thinking about itself. "Intolerable" is what it chooses not to tolerate. What is intolerable is what people do not wish—or think—to tolerate. (2) There is no equivalence of causes and effects. Suppressions, restrictions, taxes imposed by one ruler on one people at one time are not the same when imposed on other people or even on the same people at another time. It depends on *how* they think about their rulers and about themselves, and *when*. (Under Hitler many Germans—the most educated people in the world at that time—thought that they were freer than they had been before.) (3) In life, in our histories, there are "effects" that may, at times, even precede "causes": for instance, the fear (or anticipation) that something may or may not happen may cause it to happen (whence a view of "a future" may cause "a present").

In sum, mechanical causality is insufficient to understand the functioning of our minds, and consequently of our lives, and even the sense and the meaning of our memories, of the past, of history. Every human action, every human thought is something *more* than a reaction. (That is, too, how and why history never repeats itself.) The human mind intrudes into, it complicates the very structure of events.*

To this let me add my own conclusion: that this relationship, this intrusion of Mind into Matter is not constant; that perhaps the evolution of human consciousness may be the only evolution there is: and that in this age of democracy this intrusion of mind into matter tends to *increase*.† That is a startling paradox, a devel-

---

*Tocqueville saw and described this clearly in his *The Old Regime*, without philosophizing about it: that revolutions emerge not when oppression by a regime is most severe but when it has begun appreciably to lessen. (Again: "intolerable" is *what* people *no longer* want to tolerate: in other words, *when* they begin to think and *say* that this or that must not be tolerated.)

†Whence the structure of many of my books. In some of them my chapters follow each other according to a (my) ascending hierarchy: from economic to social and political and to mental, intellectual, spiritual and religious developments, from what I consider as less to what I consider more significant; that is, from the material measures of people's lives to what (and how) their thoughts and beliefs appeared and formed. (The recent and rather late-coming interest in the study of the history of *mentalités* represents a stumbling toward such recognitions, "pursuing the obvious with the enthusiasm of shortsighted detectives" [Wilde] or, rather: pursuing it with the trendy ambitions of academics.)

opment at the same time when the applications of mechanical causality govern the lives of mankind more than ever before. Wendell Berry wrote (in 1999): "It is easy for me to imagine that the next great division of the world will be between people who wish to live as creatures and people who wish to live as machines."

■

Mind over matter; mind dominating matter. Is this nothing more than a categorical assertion of a philosophy of idealism?

Yes: the opposite of materialism is idealism. But any intelligent idealist *must* be a realist. The opposite of idealism is materialism, not realism. But a categorical denial of the importance of matter is not only wrong but dangerous. Idealists understand the primacy of mind over matter, but they must recognize matter; indeed, they must be grateful for its existence. (Or to God for it: because both man and matter are God's creations.) A friar once said to the fifteenth-century German mystic Meister Eckhart: "I wish I had your soul in my body." Whereupon Eckhart: "That would be useless. A soul can save itself only in its own appointed body." A German poet, much later: "I have a great awe of the human body, for the soul is inside it." Another German philosopher (Romano Guardini): Man is not "the creature that idealism makes of him" (*At the End of the Modern World*).

I cited Germans on purpose: because there are great and grave dangers in categorical idealism, as there are in categorical materialism. There is the—frequently German, but also at times

Russian—tendency to, or belief in, an idealistic determinism. That was the essence of Hitler's National Socialist ideology: that because the ideas of National Socialists were so much stronger and better than those of their reactionary or liberal or Communist opponents, they were bound, inevitably, to triumph.*

Wrong, in this sense, are not only applications of Hegel's Zeitgeist. Wrong, too, was the English "idealist" historian R. C. Collingwood (sometimes referred to as a pioneer of "postmodernism"), who wrote that history is nothing but the history of ideas. But: no idea exists without the person who thinks it and represents it.

It took me, an antimaterialist idealist, perhaps forty or fifty years to recognize, suddenly, that people do not *have* ideas: they *choose* them.

And *how* and *why* and *when* (important, that!) they choose them:

---

*Hitler was an idealist determinist. In 1940 he said that because of the superior strength of his ideology a German soldier was worth two or three French or British or Russian soldiers, just as before 1933 National Socialist street fighters were tougher than Socialist or Communist street fighters in Germany. National Socialism was bound to triumph then and there, just as Germany was bound to triumph in this war: a repetition of what happened before, on a larger scale. His faithful adjutant General Alfred Jodl in November 1943: "We will win because we must win, for otherwise world history will have lost its meaning." Field Marshal Walter Model on *29 March 1945* (!): "In our struggle for the ideals (*Ideenwelt*) of National Socialism . . . it is a mathematical [!] certainty that we will win, as long as our beliefs and will remain unbroken."

ah! there is the crux of the matter, of men's predicaments, of their destinies, of history.

There is a deep difference between a merely antimaterialist idealism and a realistic idealism that includes the coexistence and the confluence of matter and spirit.* Whence another duality, the perennial paradox of two different tendencies existing at the same time. Yes, now: when there is obvious and present danger of people succumbing entirely to materialism. Yet a deeper and greater danger exists that may burgeon and blossom forth from false idealisms and fake spiritualisms of many kinds—from a spiritual thirst or hunger that arises at the end of an age, and that materialism cannot satisfy.

■

Still, I am not a prophet, I am a historian. We live forward, but we can think only backward (Kierkegaard). The past contains all that we know.† The "present" is a fleeting illusion; the "future" a

---

*Another neoidealist, the English Michael Oakeshott: "History is the historian's experience. It is 'made' by nobody save the historian: to write history is the only way of making it." This is separating the idea of history from history: the past from the memory of a past and from the reconstruction of some of it with the help of a historian's ideas about it, which, according to Oakeshott, alone is "history."

†Diary (hereafter D.) 14 September 2004. "Famous bromide by L. P. Hartley: 'The past is a foreign country; they do things differently there.' A classic half-truth. (Perhaps even less than half.)"

sense into which we can only project, "pre-dict," this or that known from an evolving past. History is not the entire past; but it is more than the recorded past (which is what so many people and academic historians think it is); it is the recorded and the remembered past. Like memory, it is incomplete and fallible. Memory and thinking, like imagination and seeing, are inseparable. They have their limits: but our recognition of their limits, paradoxically, may enrich us. Such is human nature. Such must be the understanding of any old or new kind of humanism—historical, rather than "scientific."

In the eighteenth century, when professional historianship first began to appear, people began to read more and more history, reading it as a form of literature. In the nineteenth century history became regarded as a science. That word, like *scientist*, had different meanings in different countries and in different languages, but let that go. It is sufficient to say that historians, many, though not all of them professionals, made immense and important contributions to historical knowledge during that century and the next. In the twentieth century the professional study of history broadened, dealing with subjects and people previously untouched. In 1694 the first edition of the *Dictionary of the French Academy* defined history as "the narration of actions and matters worth remembering." In 1935 the eighth edition said much the same: "the accounts of acts, of events, of matters worth remembering." *Dignes de mémoire*! Worth remembering! What nonsense this is! Is the historian the kind of person whose training qualifies him to tell ordinary people what is worth re-membering, to label or authenticate persons or events as if they were fossil fish or pieces of rock? Is there such a thing as a person and another such thing as a historical person? Every source is a historical source; every person is a historical person.

Whatever the *Dictionary of the French Academy* said, some French historians in the early twentieth century were extending the fields and the horizons of their historical researches. Still the cul-tural and civilizational crisis of the twentieth century affected the state and the study of history, as it affected every other art and science. Furthered by the bureaucratization of professional historianship, the essence of the trouble remained the misconception of history as a "science"—perhaps as a social science, but as a science nonetheless—including science's desideratum of the perfection of Objectivity.

At the very end of the nineteenth century one of its finest historians, Lord Acton, claimed and declared that the science of history had reached a stage when, say, a history of the Battle of Waterloo could be written that would not only be perfectly ac-ceptable to French and British and Dutch and Prussian histori-ans alike, but that would be unchanging, perennial, forever *fixed*. That was an illusion. (John Cardinal Newman once said that Acton "seems to me to expect from History more than History can furnish.") A century later we have (or ought to have) a more chas-tened and realistic view of historical and scientific Objectivity—indeed, of truth. Acton believed that history was a supremely important matter—yes—and that the purpose of history is the definite, and final, establishment of truths—no. The purpose of historical knowledge is the reduction of untruth.* (And the method of history is description, not definition.)

And such is (or should be) the purpose of every science too.

Truth is of a higher order than Justice (this primacy is there in the difference between the Old and the New Testaments). Pure Truth (again Kierkegaard) is the property of God alone: what is given to us is the pursuit of truth.† History reveals to us human fallibilities, which include the variations, the changeability and relativity of human and particular knowledge—hence the pursuit of truth, so often through a jungle of untruths. Near the end of the eighteenth century Edmund Burke saw and stated this historic condition. In the second half of the twentieth century liberal or neoconservative philosophers proposing Open Societies or Absolute Truths (Karl Popper, Leo Strauss) accused and attacked history for its "relativism." They were ignorant of the essential dif-

---

*"We find no absolute perfection in this world; always there is a background of imperfection behind our achievement; and so it is that our guesses at the truth can never be more than light obscured by shadow. The humble man's knowledge of himself is a surer way to God than any deep researches into truth." "How Truth Is to Be Learned," Chapter 3 in Thomas à Kempis's *The Imitation of Christ.*

†The purpose of law, too, must be the reduction of injustices but not a completion or perfection of justice (something to which Americans may be particularly inclined), an insane effort that may destroy men and much of the world.

ference between historicism and historicity: the first being the (mostly German and idealist) categorical concept of history, the second the recognition of the historicity of human reasoning.

The evolution is from rationalism to historicism to historicity, from the propositions of objective knowledge to that of subjective knowledge to that of personal and participant knowledge—all matters of the conscious and not of the subconscious mind. This is why at this time,* at the beginning of the twenty-first century, we must begin to think about thinking itself.

■

From dualities of human nature, to dualities of history, and to dualities of our world.

At first sight—or, rather, on the wide surface—it seems that we have entered into a world where traditions in learning are disappearing. One consequence of this is the diminution, and sometimes the elimination, of the teaching of history in schools,

---

*Time, including nonhistoric time, is a mystery deeper than that of "space" (God's creation of time being a condition of mankind, something with which Saint Augustine grappled). Among many other things, it suggests an answer to the perennial problem of human evil, which is not only that no human being has been *absolutely* evil or *absolutely* good, but that this is not a question of proportions. Was (or is) this or that evildoer, seen at times as being good to children, loyal to his friends, etc., only this or that much evil? No: this is not a question of percentages. It is that no human being can be good or evil *at the same time*—more precisely: *in the same moment.*

reducing the requirement of history courses in colleges and universities. There is, too, much evidence of the ignorance of even a basic knowledge of history among large populations in this age of mass democracy and popular sovereignty.

At the same time—and not far beneath the surface—there is another, contrary development. There are multiple evidences of an interest in, nay, of an appetite for history that has reached masses of people untouched by such before. The evidences of such appetites are so various and so many that it would take pages merely to list them, which I regret that I cannot here do.* Nor is this the place to speculate what the sources of this widespread and inchoate interest in and appetite for history might be. Of course such appetites may be easily fed with junk food. But my interest here is the appetite, not its nutrition.

---

*One (but only one) evidence: histories, of all kinds, now sell better and reach more readers than do novels. This is interesting, because in the eighteenth century professional history and the modern novel appeared around the same time, and because until about fifty years ago, vastly more people read novels than they read histories. Many of these novels were "historical novels," a genre that appeared first about two hundred years ago, employing history as a background to a novel. But worth noticing now are the interests of more and more novelists in history, whence they confect novels in which history is the main theme, the foreground. That most of them do this very badly (indeed, illegitimately: attributing nonexistent acts and words and thoughts and desires to men and women who really existed) is not my point: my argument is the piecemeal swallowing of the novel by history.

Johan Huizinga, alone, saw this duality more than seventy years ago. He was despondent about mass democracy and populism and Americanization and technology. He wrote in his debate with the French rationalist Julien Benda in 1933: "Our common enemy is the fearful master, the spirit of technology. We must not underestimate its power." Around the very time (1934) he also wrote: "Historical thinking has entered our very blood."

■

It is arguable that the two greatest intellectual achievements of the now ended age of five hundred years have been the invention (invention, rather than discovery) of the scientific method, and the development of historical thinking. Towering, of course, above the recognition of the latter stood and stands the recognition of the importance of "science," because of the fantastic and still increasing variety of its practical applications. Yet there is ample reason to recognize evidences of an increasing duality in our reactions to its ever more astonishing successful and successive applications.

At first (or even second) sight the rapid increase of the variety of the technical applications of "science" are stunning. Most of these have gone beyond even the vividest imaginations of our forebears. That they are beneficial in many fields, perhaps foremost in applications of medicine and techniques of surgery, leaves little room for doubt. That most people, including youngsters, are eager to acquire and to use the ever more complicated gadgets and machines available to them cannot be doubted either. Consider here how the natural (*natural* here means instinctive but not insightful) ability in dealing with push-button mechanical devices is normal for young, sometimes even very young, people who do not at all mind comparing or even imagining themselves as akin to those machines, unaware as they are of the complexity and the uniqueness of human nature.

At the same time consider how the reactions of people to the ever more and more complicated machines in their lives are increasingly passive. Few of them know how their machines are built and how they actually function. (Even fewer of them are capable of repairing them.) Inspired by them they are not. (Compare, for example, the popular enthusiasm that followed Lindbergh's first flight across the Atlantic in 1927 with the much weaker excitement that followed the astronauts' first flight to the moon and back forty-two years later.) Machines may make people's physical lives easier, but they do not make their thinking easier. I am not writing about happiness or unhappiness but about thinking. It is because of thinking, because of the inevitable mental intrusion into the structure and sequence of events, that the entire scheme of mechanical causality is insufficient. Still every one of our machines is wholly, entirely, dependent on mechanical causality. Yes, we employ our minds when—meaning: before, during, and after—we use them: but their functioning is entirely dependent on the very same causes producing the very same effects. It is because of their mechanical causality that computers are more than two hundred and fifty years old, indeed, outdated. In 1749 a French rationalist, De la Mettrie, wrote a famous book: *Man a Machine*. That *was* a new proposition then (though perhaps even then not much more than one of those Ideas Whose Time Has Come): dismiss soul or spirit; man may be a very complicated, perhaps the most complicated machine, but a machine nevertheless. Two hundred and fifty years later there is something dull and antiquated in such a picture: a dusty and mouldy model of human nature. Hence, below the surface: our present passive (and sometimes sickish and unenthusiastic) dependence on and acceptance of many machines.

At this stage of my argumentation someone may ask: are these not merely the opinions of an old-fashioned humanist? A poet or even a historian of a particular kind may see the realities of the world otherwise from how (and why) a natural scientist may see them. They represent Two Cultures, a humanistic and a scientific one. That was the argument of a public intellectual and a popular scientist, C. P. (later Lord) Snow, around 1960. Readers: he was wrong. There may be dualities in our reactions: but—more important—there is evidence, and increasing evidence, that the dual division of the world ever since Descartes et al. into Objects and Subjects, into Known and Knower, is no longer valid. And such evidence is not only there in, relevant to, the so-called humanities. During the general crisis at the end of an age, in the twentieth century evidence for this has been there in physics, too, involving the very study of matter.

■

Having now less than a *quart d'heure,* I must sum up the *what?* before the *how?*

Whether we call it Uncertainty or Indeterminacy or Complementarity; whether we refer to quantum physics or nuclear physics or subatomic physics or particle physics, their practitioners found that the behavior of small particles (for instance, of electrons) is considerably unpredictable; and that this kind of uncertainty is not a result of inadequately precise measurements but may be proved by experiments.

When it comes to such small particles, their observation interferes with them. Due to this human participation, their complete or "objective" definition is not possible.

They may be described (rather than "defined"), but description, too, is constrained by the limitations of human language. The very definitions of words such as *position* or *velocity* are necessarily indefinite, incomplete, and variable, dependent on the moments and conditions of their observation. (So are the mathematical formulations of their relationships.)

A fundamental unit of matter is neither measurable nor ascertainable. Does such a unit "really" exist? Even atoms and electrons are not immutable "facts." (We cannot see them. At best, we can see traces of their motions—but only with the help of machines invented by men.)

Neither are the earlier scientific distinctions between the categories of "organic" and "inorganic" matter any longer watertight.

"Energy" may be transformed into matter or heat or light: but energy is a potentiality. An accurate definition, a measurement of the temperature of an atom is impossible, because its very "existence" is only a "potentia," a probability.

In quantum physics, involving small particles, mechanical causality, as well as the complete separation of object from subject, of the knower from the known, cannot and does not apply.

■

This is a very short list of some of the more important discoveries (or rather, inventions) of quantum physics. All I hope is that some of my readers will recognize that they correspond with how we think about history—that is, with the knowledge human beings have not of things but of other human beings, involving the inevitable presence of participation.

But have historians preceded physicists with their wisdom? Oh no. The science of history, professional historianship, historians thought and said for a long time, must deal with what actually happened. That is the closest English translation of the dictum, or at least of the desideratum, that Leopold von Ranke, more than 120 years ago, stated in a famous phrase: history must be written (or taught) *wie es eigentlich gewesen,* "as it (actually, or really) happened." We ought not criticize Ranke: at that time, for his time, he was largely right. But within this phrase there lurks an illusion of a perennial definitiveness (as in Acton's earlier mentioned desideratum and illusion about a fixed, and thus forever valid, history of Waterloo). Yet the historian must always keep in mind the potentiality: that this or that may have happened otherwise.*

I happen to be a beneficiary of this. The modest success of two books I wrote, *The Duel* (1990) and *Five Days in London* (2000), dealing with May and June in 1940, has been largely due to my description of how difficult Churchill's position was in those dramatic days and weeks—a description that is inseparable from the recognition of how easily it could have been otherwise, that is, of how close Hitler was to winning the war then and there. This is but one example, one illustration of the condition that every historical actuality includes a latent potentiality. (Also: that human

*In the twentieth century Huizinga went ahead of Ranke. "The sociologist, etc., . . . simply searches for the way in which the result was already determined in the facts. The historian, on the other hand, must always maintain towards his subject an indeterminist point of view. He must constantly put himself at a point in the past at which the know factors still seem to permit different outcomes. If he speaks of Salamis, then it must be as if the Persians might still win" (*The Idea of History*).

characteristics, including mental ones, are not categories but tendencies).*

■

History is larger than science, since science is part of history and not the other way around. First came nature, then came man, and then the science of nature. No scientists, no "science."

Whence I must sum up something about the recent history of physics. The 1920s were a—so-called—golden age of physics when the recognitions of quantum physics were born, in a decade which was already chock full with the symptoms of the general cultural and civilizational crisis of the twentieth century. But then, after the Second World War, that general and profound and sickening crisis of an entire civilization, of its intellect and its arts began to envelop physics too.

How? Why? Because physicists, too, are human beings, with

---

*An—alas, trendy and unreasonable—awareness of the relations between actuality and potentiality has recently become a fad even among—again, alas—reputed historians. This fad, and the term, is that of "counterfactual" history. Both words, *factual* and *counter*, are wrong. History does not consist of "facts." And the alternative of an event is not necessarily "counter" to it, that is, its actual opposite. Indeed, the positing or suggesting alternative events must be *close* to it, *plausible*. To write a speculative "history" of what would have happened if Lee had won the battle of Gettysburg is one thing; to write another one in which the South won because a Patagonian army had arrived in Pennsylvania to help fight the North, would be quite another one, implausible and senseless.

their talents and shortcomings, with their strengths and weaknesses. During their golden age of the 1920s some of them thought seriously about what their new discoveries (or, perhaps more precisely: their new inventions) meant for human knowledge itself. As time went on (and as their reputations increased) fewer of them directed their attentions to that larger question. Heisenberg was among these few. Thirty years after his sudden pioneer and revolutionary formulation of the realities of quantum physics, and after the revolutionary and dramatic events of the Second World War, in 1955 he delivered the Gifford Lectures, amounting to his summation of what this new physics meant to our knowledge of the world. Many of his sentences were memorable. Among other things he stated that the scientific method has become its own limitation, since science by its intervention alters the objects of its investigations, "methods and objects can no longer be separated." And: "The object of research is no longer nature itself, but man's investigation of nature." Note these two words, appearing in these two separate statements: *no longer.*

Yet there were and are very few scientists who agreed or who were interested in Heisenberg's epistemological statements.* And

---

*Epistemology is (or, rather, was) a branch of philosophy dealing with theories and conditions of knowledge. I happen to believe that we have now reached a stage in the evolution of our consciousness where *all* meaningful philosophy must become epistemology. (Or, as I wrote often: we must begin thinking about thinking itself.)

during the last twenty years of his life, Heisenberg too was moving, as were most other physicists,* to seek a mathematical, a formulaic, "solution" of the problem of physical knowledge, in pursuit of what is called a Unified Theory of Matter (or, by some, a Theory of Everything). Another quarter-century later a number of physicists began to encompass absurdities.† The decline of physics began.

All of this happened during and after three quarters of a century when physicists, inventing and relying on more and more powerful machines, have found‡ more and more smaller and

---

*D. 13 April 2007. "Heisenberg was a much greater physicist than Einstein (about whom even now giant ambitious biographies are written in America). Yet not *exceptionally* great, Heisenberg. Of course Newton, Galileo, etc., were not, either."

†There are many examples of this. Here is one I now cite (not for the first time), by a Nobel Prize–winning physicist, Steven Weinberg (1999): "The universe is very large, and it should be no surprise that, among the enormous number of planets that support only unintelligent life and the still vaster number of planets that cannot support life at all, there is some tiny fraction on which there are living beings who are capable of thinking about the universe, as we are doing here." Whereupon I wrote: "What kind of language—and logic—is this? '*No surprise*'? Consider: The five boroughs of New York are very large, *and it should be no surprise* that, among the enormous number of its inhabitants who do not walk and the still vaster number who do not like to walk at all, there is some tiny fraction who are able to levitate."

‡*Found* is not really a good word, because it may be argued that their findings have been inventions rather than discoveries.

smaller particles of matter affixing them with all kinds of names—until now, well into the twenty-first century, it is (or should be) more and more likely that not only A Basic Theory of Everything but that the smallest Basic Unit of Matter will and can never be found. And why? Because these particles are produced by scientists, human beings themselves.

Every piece of matter, including the smallest—just as every number—is endlessly, infinitely divisible because of the human mind. Some scientists will admit this. Others won't.

What science amounts to is a probabilistic kind of knowledge with its own limits, due to the limitations of the human mind, including the mental operations and the personal characters of scientists themselves, their potentialities ranging from sublime to fallible. There is only one kind of knowledge, human knowledge, with the inevitability of its participation, with the inevitable relationship of the knower to the known, of what and how and why and when man knows and wishes to know.

■

This has always been so—even as the recognitions of these conditions have varied.

But now, in the twenty-first century, at the end of the "modern" age, something new, something unprecedented has come about. For the first time since Adam and Eve, for the first time in the history of mankind, men have acquired the power to destroy much of the earth and much of mankind, potentially even most of it.

At the beginning of the Modern Age, some five centuries ago, Bacon wrote: Knowledge is Power. Near the end of this age we know, or ought to know, that the increase of power—including mental power—tends to corrupt.

Until now the great earth-shattering catastrophes—earthquakes, floods, firestorms, pests, plagues, epidemics—came from the outside. Now the potential dangers are coming from the inside: Nuclear explosions, global warming, new kinds of contaminations, pestilences produced by mankind itself (for instance by genetic engineering).* All of such dangers come from men's increasing knowledge—or, rather, from his increasing interference with elements of "nature." There may be a shift now, from the potential dangers of material technology to biotechnology.

Of course a "danger" is a potentiality, not an actuality. Of course some of these developments may not happen. The road to hell may be paved with good intentions: but the road to

---

*In other words: mind leading to matter, mind preceding matter. The very history of medicine, the etiology (meaning: the study of the sources) of illnesses, is a startling proof of this. Especially among the most "advanced" peoples of the modern world, an increasing number and variety of illnesses now come not from outside, not from wounds or infections, but from the "inside"—another evidence of the increasing intrusion of mind, of the sometimes palpable but in essence deep and complex—confluences of mind and matter in human lives.

heaven too may be paved with bad intentions that have not matured into acts. That is our saving grace, our hope. But we must recognize the sources of our new and enormous dangers: not outside us but inside this world, because of the minds of men, including "scientists" and those who support and cheer them on.* We must rethink the very idea and meaning of "progress."

And now a step—a last step—further. We must recognize, we must understand, that we are at the center of the universe.

---

*An illustration. "It has become part of accepted wisdom [?] to say that the twentieth century was the century of physics and the twenty-first century will be the century of biology. Two facts [?] about the coming century are agreed on by almost anyone [?]. Biology is now bigger than Physics. . . . These facts [?] raise an interesting question. Will the domestication of high technology, which we have seen marching from triumph to triumph with the advent of personal computers and GPS receivers and digital cameras, soon be extended from physical technology to biotechnology? I believe that the answer to this question is yes. Here, I am bold enough to make a definite prediction. I predict that the domestication [?] of biotechnology will dominate our lives during the next fifty years at least as much as the domestication of computers has dominated our lives during the previous fifty years."

Thus begins the leading article in the 19 July 2007 number of the *New York Review of Books*—"many of his essays appeared in these pages"—by Freeman Dyson, Professor of Physics Emeritus at the Institute for Advanced Study in Princeton. "Accepted wisdom." "Facts." "Domestication." Thus an idiot savant.

■

Contrary to all accepted ideas we must now, at the end of an age, at the beginning of a new one, understand and recognize that *we* and *our earth* are at the center of our universe.*

We did not *create* the universe. But the universe is our *invention:* and, as are all human and mental inventions, time-bound, relative, and potentially fallible.

Because of this recognition of the human limitations of theories, indeed, of knowledge, this assertion of our *centrality*—in other words, of a new, rather than renewed, anthropocentric and geocentric view of the universe—is not arrogant or stupid. To the contrary: it is anxious and modest. Arrogance and stupidity, or at best shortsightedness, are the conditions of those who state that what human beings have figured out (most of these figurations occurring during the past five hundred years, a short period in the history of mankind!)—that water *is* H_2O, that there *cannot* be speed greater than 186,262 mph, that e $= mc^2$, etc., etc., that these scientific and mathematical formulas are absolute and eternal truths, everywhere and at any time in the universe, trillions of years ago as well as trillions of years in the future; that mathematics and geometry preceded the existence of our world—that these are eternally valid facts or truths even before the universe

*D. 1 May 2001. "John Polkinghorne [religious physicist at Cambridge] in *Religion and Science:* he wants to square the circle. I want to circle the circle."

existed and even if and when our world or, indeed, the universe will cease to exist.

No. The known and visible and measurable conditions of the universe are not *anterior* but *consequent* to our existence and to our consciousness. The universe is such as it is because at the center of it there exist conscious and participant human beings who can see it, explore it, study it.* This insistence on the centrality, and on the uniqueness of human beings is a statement not of arrogance but of humility. It is yet another recognition of the inevitable limitations of mankind.

I ask my readers to hear my voice. It is an appeal (*appeal: call: ring*) to think—yes, at a certain stage of history. I can only hope that for some people the peal may ring with at least a faint echo of truth. It is an appeal to the common sense of my readers.

When I, a frail and fallible man, say that every morning the sun comes up in the east and goes down in the west, I am not lying. I do not say that a Copernican or post-Copernican astronomer, stating the opposite, that the earth goes around the sun, is lying. There is accuracy, determinable, provable accuracy in his assertions: But my commonsense experience about the sun and the earth is both prior to and more basic than any astronomer's formula.

Keep in mind that all prevalent scientific concepts of matter, and

---

*For those readers who believe in God: the world, and this earth were created by Him for the existence and consciousness of human beings.

of the universe, are *models*. A model is man-made, dependent on its inventor. A model cannot, and must not, be mistaken for the world.

And now there exists an additional, and very significant, evidence of our central situation in the universe. Five centuries ago, the Copernican / Keplerian / Galilean / Cartesian / Newtonian discovery—a real discovery, a real invention, a calculable and demonstrable and provable one—removed us and the earth from the center of the universe. (Often with good intentions.) Thereafter, with the growth of scientism, and especially with the construction of ever more powerful instruments, among them telescopes (instruments separating ourselves ever more from what we can see with our naked eyes: but of course the human eye is never really "naked"), this movement led to our and to our earth having become less than a speck of dust at the rim of an enormous dustbin of a universe, with the solar system itself being nothing more than one tiniest whirl among innumerable galaxies. But the physicists' (perhaps especially Niels Bohr's) recognition that the human observer cannot be separated from things he observes (especially when it comes to the smallest components of matter) reverses this. We and the earth on and in which we live, are back at the center of the universe*—a universe which is—unavoidably—an anthropocentric and geocentric one.

---

*D. 20 December 2005. "All right: my knowledge that we on this earth are at the center of the universe, which (of course) is our invention. We have been inventing (and re-inventing) the universe. But God is more than our invention.

This is something other than the returning movement of a pendulum. History, and our knowledge of the world, swings back, but not along the arc where it once was. It is due to our present historical and mental condition that we must recognize, and proceed from a chastened view of ourselves, of our situation, at the center of *our* universe. For *our* universe is not more or less than *our* universe.* That has been so since Adam and Eve, including Ptolemy, Copernicus, Galileo, Newton, Einstein, Heisen-

---

And to those who think that God is nothing but our invention my question is: Why? What makes human beings want such an invention? Is it not that a spark *of God may exist within us?"*

*Already more than four hundred years ago Montaigne wrote: "The question is whether if Ptolemy was therein deceived, upon the foundations of his reason, it were not very foolish to treat now in what these later people [the "Copernicans"] say: and whether it is not more likely that this great body, which we call the world, is not quite another thing than that what we imagine." And another fifty years later, Pascal, a different thinker from Montaigne: "Thought constitutes the greatness of man." "Man is but a reed . . . but he is a thinking reed. The entire universe need not arm itself to crush him. A vapor, a drop of water suffices to kill him. But if the universe were to crush him, man would still be more noble than that which killed him, because he knows that he dies and the advantage which the universe has over him; the universe knows nothing of this. All our dignity consists, then, in thought. By it we must elevate ourselves, and not by space and time which we cannot fill." "*A thinking reed.* It is not from space that I must seek my dignity, but from the government of my thought. I shall have no more if I possess worlds. By space the universe encompasses and swallows me up like an atom; by thought I comprehend the world."

berg, and my own dual, because human (opinionated as well as humble), self.*

Our thinking of the world, our imagination (and we imagine and see together) anthropomorphizes and humanizes everything, even inanimate things, just as our exploration of the universe is inevitably geocentric. It is not only that "Know Thyself" is the necessary fundament of our understanding of other human beings. It is, too, that we can never go wholly outside of ourselves, just as we can never go outside the universe to see it.

■

In sum. Our consciousness, our central situation in space, cannot be separated from our consciousness of time.[†] Does it not, for example, behoove Christian believers to think that the coming of Christ to this earth may have been *the* central event of the uni-

---

*D. 13 January 2006. "In the end my quick but strong vision that we are at the center of the universe, etc., has been—perhaps—an important recognition. Whether it will be later discovered by admirers does not matter. What matters, alas, is that I threw these things, these recognitions, off, without much insisting and developing and propagating them. This happened (and still happens) because of the frivolousness and failures of my character. My 'historical' philosophy, this new monism of our knowledge of ourselves and of the universe, may be my great mental achievement. But I do not feel particularly proud of this."

†D. 18 April 2007. "Heidegger, *Dasein*, etc. 'Any description of consciousness must include a world.' No: any description of a world must include consciousness—of one's own perspective, of one's time, of one's situation in history, etc."

verse: that the most consequential event in the entire universe has occurred here, on this earth two thousand years ago? Has the son of God visited this earth during a tour of stars and planets, making a spectacular Command Performance for different audiences, arriving from some other place and—perhaps—going off to some other place?

And only two thousand years ago. The arguments of Creationism against Evolutionism entirely miss this essential matter. That is the unavoidable contradiction not between "Evolution" and "Creation" but between evolution and history. History: because in the entire universe we are the only historical beings. Our lives are not automatic; we are responsible for what we do, say, and think. The coming of Darwinism was historical, appearing at a time of unquestioned Progress. But its essence was, and remains, antihistorical. It elongated the presence of mankind to an ever-increasing extent, by now stretching the first appearance of "man" on this earth to more than a million years—implying that consequently there may be something like another million years to come for us. Ought we not question this kind of progressive optimism—and, at a time when men are capable of altering nature here and there and of destroying much of the world, including many of themselves?

∎

Such is my sketch of a new architecture of humanism, of a chastened humanism cognizant of our unavoidable limitations, and of the earth and ourselves being at the center of the universe, *our* universe. What an ambitious proposition! And isn't ambition inseparable from vanity? Why did I place this at the beginning of a kind of autobiography that ought to be not much more than an entertaining account, an ambling *causerie*?

TWO

Why?

Why? is a complex question, since it is twofold. It involves motives and purposes, past and future: the "why?" of *because,* and the "why?" of *wherefore?* Here I am concerned with the second of these, with the purpose, not the motive. What am I writing for? For what? For whom? What reason is there to write a second volume of confessions, about myself in the past twenty years, near the end of my life? Why should that be of interest to thousands of readers, including even those few who happen to be aware of me and my work? Asking this is not a result of humility or of modesty. Knowing this almost stopped me from beginning such a book at all.

Almost: but not quite. An entry in my diary, 18 January 2007, when I was struggling with how to begin this book: "Heisenberg, shortly before his death (1976): 'the hope, that from now on a newer, further way of thinking may start, [something] that at this time may be felt rather than described.' Well, I *am* describing the gist of it. However: I have written about some of these important matters before, here and there. So: does my summing up this gist in *Last Rites* make much or any sense? What is it that I can tell in such a second book of an autobiography that would interest people and be therefore worth while?"

A newer, further way of thinking—described, not just felt?

So I went on—very much aware, among other things, of the marvelous complexity of the relationship of *why?* to *how?* Often, if not indeed always, the *why?* is already implicit in the *how*. If I am taking a liberty—and it is a liberty—to write something at my old age,* this better be interesting and different from what I wrote about myself at sixty-five. Whether this will work will depend on the *how*, which is a question unimaginable and inadmissible to any machine or computer. The computer responds neither to the *how* nor to the *why*. All it can spit out is: *what*.

■

I was—I still am—a man of the twentieth century, born in 1924, ten years after the historical twentieth century began.[†] It was a short century of seventy-five years, from 1914 to 1989, its land-

---

*D. 21 May 2007: " 'In old age 'one's face is to the wall' (Iris Origo). Fairly so, but, thank God, not quite."

[†]I was born on 31 January 1924, seven days after Lenin died and two days before Woodrow Wilson died. Often, and for long, I have seen these two revolutionaries, that half-Tartar and that horse-faced professor, as nineteenth-century brains.

scape dominated by two enormous mountain ranges: the First World War that led to the Second World War that led to the cold war, ending in 1989. Another coincidence: it was around 1989 that some important matters in my life too changed. I am aware now, as I was aware then, that a new century, the twenty-first, had begun, to which I do not and shall not belong. But I was aware of something greater and longer too: that an entire civilization, the European era of five hundred years, that I cherished and to which I belonged, was gone.* Dribs and drabs of it may still live here and there. That is not a contradiction: that is how history proceeds. Georges Bernanos wrote that "a civilization disappears with the kind of man, the type of humanity, that has issued from it." Well, I have not wholly disappeared, I live still. No contradiction here either, only the mercy of God.

"Diary of a Despairing Man," *Tagebuch eines Verzweifelten*, was the title of the diary of a lonely German reactionary, Friedrich von Reck-Malleczewen, during Hitler's rule of the Third Reich. That could be the title of a diary that I began in December 2000 (another coincidence) which I am keeping even now. (From it some of the footnotes of this book.).

■

It could be the title of this book too. However: *Last Rites* is better, if perhaps slightly droll. And Reck-Malleczewen wrote only that

*D. 25 December 2001. "Never did I *know* so deeply that I live now not *at the end* but *beyond* the end of an age."

diary. "Against the dark, and Time's consuming rage"? But then despair is sinful, since it is often self-indulgent. Whoa! Isn't any autobiography self-indulgent?* Yes it is; and qui s'excuse s'accuse; but at least I think I know what to avoid.

There is this odd thing. Historians' autobiographies are almost always bad. They range from Unsatisfactory to Wretched.

The Autobiography of Edward Gibbon is no exception. It is supposed to be a classic, in print for more than two hundred years, republished in The World's Classics and in Everyman's Library, etc., etc. There are a few good passages in it, but it is pompous and chortling: "That I am equal or superior to some [other] biographers, the effects of modesty or affectation cannot force me to dissemble." It is all about Gibbon's private life; but very little of what is private.† These are the ruminations of a man who has grown old and fat. He decided to write it after his really immortal *Decline and Fall:* Yet, except for one famous passage about when and how the idea of writing *Decline and Fall* came to his mind on 15 October 1764, in Rome, there is very little about his plan and composition and execution of that marvelous and magisterial and, in its way, pathbreaking work. So: why did he

---

*D. 11 February 2001. "What an egotistic practice a diary is."

D. 5 September 2005. "Jim Lees-Milne once wrote that diaries written for oneself are necessarily morbid and self-indulging; that one should write one's diaries (if at all) as if they are written for one's great-grandchild. Much truth in that."

†In *Decline and Fall* he wrote here and there with gusto about courtesans; but as Philip Guedalla once put it: "Gibbon lived out his sex life in his footnotes."

begin writing an autobiography in the fifty-second year of his life? "I now propose to employ some moments of my leisure in reviewing the simple transactions of a private and literary life. Truth—naked, unblushing truth, the first virtue of more serious history—must be the sole recommendation of this personal narrative." Naked, unblushing truth is nowhere in this book. Except—perhaps—at its very end, where he ruminates ("ruminates" *is* the proper verb)* with what Fontenelle and Voltaire had written about "autumnal felicity": he is "more inclined to embrace than to dispute this comfortable doctrine . . . but I must reluctantly observe that two causes, the abbreviation of time and the failure of hope, will always tinge with a browner shade the evening of life." However, there are consolations of hope, including "the vanity of authors, who presume the immortality of their name and writings." Well, at least this cadence is vintage Gibbon and of the Age of Reason. Or of "browner shade," the Age of Raisin—whose sweetness he could not much taste. He died a few years later, and he never really finished his *Autobiography* which he thought would be a great little work of art.[†]

---

*D. 19 April 2007. "Gibbon: 'The use of letters is the principal circumstance that distinguishes a civilised people from a herd of savages incapable of knowledge and reflection.' People today: capable of knowledge but incapable of reflection."

[†]Several passages or versions in several chapters remained: they were put together, not very scrupulously but, by and large, very well by his friend Lord Sheffield. What I find interesting are coincidences, connections: that Gibbon was—distantly—related to Acton's grandfather; and that Suzanne Curchod, that simple, charming girl, who had taste and judgment enough to reject Gib-

Not many historians have written their autobiographies. One day a thoughtful and literate biographer or historian ought to compose a descriptive and comparative study of those who did. The greatest historians during the past two hundred years, Burckhardt in the nineteenth century and Huizinga in the twentieth, did not write such. Some of my contemporaries or near-contemporaries did; I read them; and found them dreadfully dull at best, or self-indulgent and therefore dishonest at their worst.*

Why is this so? Perhaps because historians had put so much of their thoughts and ideas and insights into their history writing, attempting to convince their readers (and themselves) that what they wrote was "objective" and impersonal, so that there was, or should be, no room for what is personal, or what is left? Did they have a schizophrenia of memory? Did they think more and more about the records of this or that historical past; separated from the memories of their own past?† Did they not see—or did they not wish to see—the connection? But that connection of the his-

---

bon's proposal to be engaged to him, subsequently rose high in the world to become Necker's wife.

*(A shocking example of the latter is A. J. P. Taylor's.) D. 14 December 2000. "His autobiography is dreadful, as are the reminiscences of his third wife, who keeps repeating that she and Taylor had 'good sex.' A disgusting phrase. Also: what in the past may have been a very private confession has now become a public assertion."

†Yet some of the best memoirs or fragments of memoirs that I admire had been written by superb writers of history who were not professional historians—for example, Churchill or George Kennan; add to them such nonautobiographical but, rather, autohistorical fragments by Tocqueville in his *Souvenirs*.

torical past with our own past is inevitable. Not determined: but inevitable. By "connection" I mean knowledge—and knowledge of the conscious, not of the "subconscious," mind. The conditions of knowledge, of historical knowledge, of past knowledge, of human knowledge, of my own knowledge, stir me, they make me write now this autobiography. Self-knowledge: I am a participant of history—but not only what and when and where it happened during my lifetime. Many of my books dealt with themes and events of the twentieth century—but not about what I have experienced. I know that I can have an empathy with men and women of distant pasts. As my master Huizinga once wrote: "A feeling of immediate contact with the past is a sensation as deep as the purest enjoyment of art; it is an almost ecstatic sensation . . . of touching the essence of things, of through history experiencing the truth." I was, and am, not a witness but a participant.

■

Confessions amounted to an account of the development and of the occasional crystallization of *my* thoughts and beliefs. *Last Rites* may amount to my last, desperate attempt to teach . . .

This has something—not everything but something—to do with one of the changes in my life that began about twenty years ago and came to end some years later. In 1987 I began to limit my months of teaching (in order to have more time for writing); but about seven years later I was compelled to retire from teaching altogether. I regretted this, though there was too an element of relief, since I now had much more time to write. Sixty years ago I began to teach in order to be able to write. Decades went by before I began to realize that I was a fairly good teacher. What mattered more than such an egoist realization was my recognition that my writing actually profited from my teaching undergraduates, due to the constant exercise to describe to them distant and often difficult events, peoples and places remote from them and from their minds, economically, simply, but not superficially.

History does not repeat itself. Alas, historians often repeat themselves. I am much aware of this. I have tried to avoid this throughout my career. Sometimes I could not. Here I must admit that in the preceding chapter of those Bad Fifteen Minutes I had to include or condense or rephrase a few phrases or passages from my earlier writings. I have a kind of excuse, also derived from teaching. Teachers *must* sometimes repeat—repeat things, not themselves—for the sake of their students. Here is a duality. Every teacher knows (and often complains) that his teaching may have been largely futile. His students not only failed to understand: they did not even *hear* what he said. And then, many years later, the shock of surprise: *what* this former student had remembered! *what* that former student had heard!

But here I am writing not for students but for readers.

■

There are dualities in every human being. And in their purposes. Here, too. Why I am writing this? Because of vanity; and of hope.

Vanity first! I am now eighty-four years old, living in comfort, though increasingly remote from the world around me. At least two dozen books I have written were published (many of them translated into other languages in other countries) in the past twenty years of my life. Much of this happened because the reputation of their readability, of the qualities and the style of their narrative prose. This should please my vanity. Whether it adds to it I do not know.

What I know—and what I fear few of my readers know—is that the very structure and even the style of my histories have been consequent to my convictions of what history and historical knowledge consist of near and at the end of a great historical age. I have now condensed these convictions into about forty pages. Why now? In 1968 my *Historical Consciousness* was published. There I had set out, in considerable (and perhaps undue) detail, a historical philosophy of history. Thirty-two years later a remote single reviewer of *Historical Consciousness* wrote that it was a forerunner, "far, far ahead of everything with what in the 1970s and 1980s historical and philosophical thinkers began to be preoccupied." I kept on thinking and speculating about historical knowledge, history and physics, etc. My compulsion to write about these matters never left me. Then I wrote *At the End of an Age* (2002), at the end of which, together with related subjects, I raised the proposition of our centrality in the universe. No attention was paid to these epistemological propositions.

But: why complain?* Twenty years ago, on the last page of *Confessions* . . . that autohistory *aetatis* 60–65, I wrote that I had had a happy unhappy life, which is preferable to an unhappy happy one. It is still now, *aetatis* 84. Thinking and thinking about these *Last Rites*, I have felt compelled to make a last attempt, a final summary, a crystallization of my, yes, radical recognitions of human and historical and physical knowledge—and to put this at the beginning, commonsensically and economically, as best I can, with a very minimum of quotes and quotations, with paragraphs potentially expandable into entire books, into a handful of pages, readable in a quarter of an hour, for all kinds of readers. Worth a try? Worth a—last—throw? Perhaps—perhaps—it won't vanish forever.

Vanitas vanitatis! Quelle vanité! What vanity this is!† I know. But next—or beneath?—vanity there sits my purpose and my faith in hope. Hope for a recognition not of my philosophic attempts, not of their formulation, but of their essence. Hope resting on my conviction of *reminder*, of the wisdom uttered by Samuel Johnson, who said that we must not instruct people but remind them, remind them of some things that they may already know but that have not—yet—surfaced to the level of their con-

---

*Péguy to Sorel (circa 1911): "You are right, but one has no right to be right unless one is willing personally to pay the price of demonstrating the rightness of the truth."

†D. 7 July 2007. "All week I worked and almost finished the philosophical portion of *Last Rites*, weighed down by the knowledge and sense of how utterly futile this may be."

sciousness. A hopeful reminder! But, as everything else, a reminder depends not only on *what?* and *how?* and *why?* but also—indeed, very much—on *when?* At this time, at the end of a great age when, having liberated mankind from all kinds of fetters, having declared the end of slavery, emancipation of women and of children, entire liberties of speech, of print, of pictures, etc., men's images of men and women are more sordid, more ugly, more desperate than ever?*

Still: *some kind* of a response to that will come. Perhaps too late. But such is the history of history.

And so, from this distillation of my thinking, and of my reasons for writing, for my purpose to remind—for which I hope my readers will forgive me—to my own autohistory, to circumstances of my life during the past twenty years I now shall turn.

---

*D. 19 May 2002. "Kierkegaard: '*Summa summarum.* The human race ceased to fear God. Then came its punishment: it began to fear itself, began to cultivate the fantastic, and now it trembles before this creature of its own imagination.' Profound and true, even truer in 2007 than in 1847 or thereabouts."

THREE

The World Around Me: My Adopted Country

Writing a history of the United States; writing *any* history of the United States; writing a history of any portion of the United States; writing a history of any portion of its past are commendable and creditable attempts: but they involve—or, rather, they ought to involve—problems that their writers ought to recognize before they begin. The history of every country is unique. But the problems of American history are special, too, because of the structure of its democratic society—and that involves the very structure of its events. The history of a democracy is more difficult to write—properly—than the history of an aristocratic or semiaristocratic nation, since it must include more than the history of a governing class and of a state, it must involve the history of a majority of a people. But: who *are* the people? What did they say? When and how did they speak? Where and what are the evidences of that? Is it not, rather, that there are people who spoke and chose and acted in the name of the people? If so, we are already one step removed from "reality." Yes, there is a vast multiplicity of records of what some people—notice: "*some* people," not "*the* people"—said and chose and did. But how did the consequent "facts," or events, come about? How did they happen; or, rather, how were they *made* to happen? The accumulation of opinions is what counts, not the accumulation of capital. But the persistent prediction of opinions may create public opinions (just as the prediction of profits leads to a rise in the price of shares). These matters are not simple. American history is not simple. I am a historian who saw some of this from the very beginning of his life in the United States, in his adopted country. I wrote about these things on occasion. I think that I could still write a little book about the peculiar problems of the approaches, of the perspectives, of the methods, of the sources of American history, of its epistemology, of its hermeneutics. Now, in addition to its democratic complications, these matters have become ever more unmanageable and confusing and obscured by the burgeoning of technology and of secrecy.* Also, popularity no

---

*D. 19 January 2001. "I never much liked the term Enlightenment, and now many of its illusions are gone. There is one exception where the word applies: the eventual opening of libraries, archives, records. Not fresh air and fresh light but more air and more light from those documents and papers. However: this too has been a passing phase. With the arrival of telecommunications of all kinds, and

longer merely *depends* on publicity; it has become *inseparable* from it. These complications now involve the liquefaction of the once categorical distinction between primary and secondary sources, because of the liquefaction of personal records, of what remains authentic and what is no longer so. There are enormous dark clouds massing above the blazing artificial lights of the people's stadia: obscureness unrecognized, unseen, unfelt by millions beneath, within the "show."

Now enough of this. I must limit myself to describing some things I saw and remember. Except for one last remark, or caveat: many things that I saw were not what many others saw. What happened was what people thought happened. I thought too that they happened: but sometimes I also thought that what happened meant something else. Usually beneath the surface: but then democratic surfaces are big and thick. Sometimes I was wrong.

■

Some time in the 1960s the behavior of many Americans changed. "Behavior" is not only superficial or external. When behavior changes, thinking changes too. There are few people in whose lives behavior and thinking are so interlaced, so dependent on each other, as in the United States, where images often not only clothe but absorb essence, where for so many people to seem is as

---

central intelligence agencies, etc., more and more things now remain and will remain unrecorded or unaccessible, unavailable, unreconstructable . . . "

important as to be. (Two examples: In no other country does the description of a person in a newspaper report or even in a serious magazine article begin with a detailed description of his clothes. Or consider how the word, or observation, of "body language" is very American, appearing first in the 1960s: a foul-smelling phrase, is it not?)

There was the duality of the sixties. During that decade all kinds of public campaigns and legal reforms were, or at least pretended to be, concerned with the extension and the protection of the rights of individual privacy. Yet it was in the 1960s that so much of the presence and even the desire of personal privacy melted away. One evidence of that was the final disappearance of "society," its substitution being the cult of celebrity.

The bourgeois, the urban, period in the history of the United States lasted approximately from 1880 to 1950. This is a very large country, and there were vast exceptions, portions untouched by it, but so it was. America and Europe (and England) grew closer. America entered two world wars to help Britain, and Western Europe. After 1880 American cities grew larger than London, Paris, Berlin. The New World was no longer the antithesis or the opposite of the Old. It became the repository of its civilization, culture, arts. It was spared the catastrophes that befell Europe in the two world wars. Its institutions represented many of the values and the standards of a constitutional and liberal order. There was an American upper class whose power and ambitions were limited, but whose prestige was extant and attractive. But the convictions of their members were regrettably superficial, and their self-confidence remarkably weak. Latest during the 1960s they dissolved and disappeared, fast.* The behavior of their offspring changed instantly, together with what and how they thought.

Suburbanization; female "emancipation";[†] civil rights for blacks; a loud cult of youth; television; a raucous sexual "revolution"; a rise of divorces, of abortions, etc., etc.,—of course they had forerunners, symptoms here and there evident in the fifties, and then much of these continued in the seventies and later: but my argument is that the sixties had two, at first sight contradictory, characteristics. Their happenings were ephemeral: but their effects were enduring. When in 1969 nearly half a million young Americans streamed to and crowded into a "festival" near Woodstock, New York, slews of disquisitions and articles declared this, breathlessly, as a revolution without precedent, with tremendous unforeseeable social and political consequences. In reality it re-

---

*D. 17 August 2004. "George Bush (the present President's father) told the American Olympic team in Athens to be sportsmanlike, to behave 'with class.' Class! that present, and stupid, usage of the word from the mouth of someone whom Americans describe—wrongly—as a 'patrician' or 'aristocrat.' This is the same man who speaks of his grandchildren as 'grandkids.' No gentleman would have ever used such a word."

[†]D. 6 June 2004. "Result of civilizational degeneration: while a young fool would still not mind it if someone would call him a gentleman, no young woman now wants to be called a lady."

sulted in nothing. What endured after the sixties were the muta-
tions of behavior, ranging from clothes to habits, of manners as
much as of morals. I am not writing this out of nostalgia for the
America of the 1940s or 1950s: for the germinating symptoms of
these changes had been already there. Then, latest in the 1960s,
the bourgeois and urban and urbane chapter in the history of the
United States of America came to its very end.*

As in so many instances this was (and still is) obscured by
the falseness of the words categorizing it—with the result of
problems wrongly stated. The enduring changes involved not
"culture" but civilization. *Civilization* is a word that appears in
English only in 1601, with its definition: "an emergence from
barbarism."† The intellectualization of the word *culture*, mostly
of German origin, came much later. The elevation of its prestige
over *civilization* has caused enormous harm, especially in the history of Germany.‡ When civilization is strong and widespread
enough, "culture" will appear and take care of itself.

---

*The real and only "modern" decade was the 1920s, not the 1960s. The lat-
ter was but the last, exaggerated, and often superficial application of the former.

†As the 1960s proceeded, with many murders, there was an ocean of aroused
concern with "violence": but the problem was not *violence*, it was *savagery*.

‡D. 27 January 2001. "Reading Englishmen and Englishwomen who were
contemporaries of Spengler, say, about 1928. Yes, they were tired, and imperial
Britain had begun to crumble. But, with all of his gigantic vision: was Spengler
more intelligent than they were? Yes and no. Or: no, rather than yes. Their way
of speaking was better than Spengler's, which was not only a matter of language

The institutionalization of rights of women, of blacks, of homosexuals, for abortion, for semipornography, for free speech* and behavior, etc., looked and still look as extensions of liberalism, more juddering jolts toward a freer, more democratic, more liberal world. In reality, liberalism was dying. Ten years after the 1960s it was just about dead. It belonged to a past; it had nothing more to achieve; it was exhausted. Its tasks had been done. It had emancipated hundreds of millions worldwide. I write *emancipated* rather than *freed*, because it is more difficult to be free than not to be free: but that is a perennial human predicament. In the United States the demise of Liberalism is clear and present in the history of words. In 1950 there was not one American public or political or academic or intellectual figure who declared himself *a* "conservative." By 1980 more Americans declared themselves "conservatives" than "liberals." They, including most professed American Christians, chose Ronald Reagan, a divorced movie actor, for their hero, for their president. This was a tectonic change in the politi-

---

but of style too. Moreover: Spengler was no triumph of character. . . . He had a Cyclopean eye. But he was much less civilized than these tired Englishmen and Englishwomen, and I do not only mean his manners (though that is also telling). They may have been—they were—over-civilized. Spengler was over-cultured. And here my deep conviction: civilization is more important than culture, esp. than 'Kultur.'"

*D. 12 May 2002. "Kierkegaard: 'People hardly ever make use of the freedom which they have, for example, freedom of thought; instead they demand freedom of speech as compensation.'"

cal history of the United States that had no precedent. But the manners and morals of most American "conservatives" hardly differed from those of most other Americans, including "liberals."*

By the 1980s the United States was, by and large, a classless society. Of course there were many poor people (as Jesus said: "the poor you will always have with you") and many newer and richer new rich; but the habitual phenomena and categories such as "middle class" and "working class" had just about lost their meanings. There was no upper class left, and the poorest were not or hardly working. There was but one kind of viscuous cement that bound the majority of this amorphous society together: the popular sentiment of nationalism.

■

More than one hundred years ago, in Europe as well as in America, Public Opinion became absorbed by popular sentiment. Those

---

*D. 29 August 2004. "I know two rigid and near-extreme conservatives in this neighborhood Their children are among the worst behaved. That too is telling."

D. 16 February 2002. "High-school students in a Kansas town stole their homework papers from the Internet and presented them entirely as their own. Their teacher, a young woman, 26, failed about twenty of them. The principal and the school board decided to restore their marks and to dismiss her. I am inclined to think that the school board people and the parents and the principal who insisted on her dismissal and on changing the students' grades are Republicans and Conservatives . . . "

who were interested in it, who attempted to identify it, ascertain it, measure it, continued to call it Public Opinion: another misuse of words. The same thing happened with the confusion of patriotism (old and traditional) with nationalism (new and democratic). I wrote about this elsewhere and I am loath to repeat myself. It may be enough to say that patriotism is defensive, while nationalism is aggressive; that patriotism means the love of a country, while nationalism is the cult of a people (and of the power of their state). Again we face the confusion of language: what Americans call a superpatriot is, in reality, a supernationalist. Throughout American history there have been many nationalist presidents; but few of them like Ronald Reagan, unabashedly so.

Then came the end of the cold war, an immediate consequence of the implosion of the Soviet Union's empire with which Ronald Reagan (contrary to popular and "conservative" beliefs) had little to do.*

I wish to record that the first reactions of the American people to the collapse of the Soviet Russian empire were commendable. There was no popular jubilation, no wish to rub Russian noses in the dust, no public proclamations (except by some Republicans that their party had "won" the cold war). But soon the tempta-

---

*D. 14 April 2003. "A Philadelphia radio personality, stupid, chauvinistic, fast-talking, calls me for a short telephone interview. He asks me: 'Come on! Hasn't Reagan single-handedly brought down the Soviet Union?' I: 'Yes, and Jefferson Davis won the Civil War.' He is furious and hangs up."

tion to extend American power into portions of the world emptied by another great power proved to be too alluring—in this case less because of popular nationalism than because of the officers of the American superstate. In this there was not much difference between Republicans and Democrats. It was the government of Clinton (a man otherwise not much interested in foreign policy) that chose to extend the American military presences into Somalia, into the Caucasus, into the Baltic, etc. At the beginning of the twenty-first century, as America's third century began, there were perhaps more than seven hundred American "bases" all around the world. I doubt whether there was, or is, a single man or woman in the Pentagon or in the Department of State (or of course in the White House) who could list even half of them. Neither could the American people, ignorant of the extent of what this means. Most of them went on believing that they are a Chosen People, an exception not only to others but to history itself, that they were living in the greatest and freest and richest country in the world. The decision of George W. Bush* and of his followers to go to war against Iraq was part and parcel of such beliefs—but with one ominous condition, perhaps without precedent. That decision was not the result of inadequate in-

---

*D. 14 September 2001. "Three days ago: the fanatics' planes smashing into the New York towers and the Pentagon. I am appalled by Bush. His first reaction: calling the perpetrators 'cowards.' Fanatics and murderers, yes. Cowards: not. Were Genghis Khan, Ivan, Hitler, etc., cowards? Alas, they were not. Bush likes the word: 'War.' Declare war, and against whom?"

telligence. (That the CIA tells presidents what they wish to hear was nothing new.) Nor was it the result of geopolitical calculation. The choice of that war was his and his advisers' belief that going into Iraq and crushing its miserable dictator in a quick war would be popular, resounding to a great and enduring advantage to his reputation and to the Republican Party's dominance in the foreseeable future.* There have been many American presidents who had chosen to go to war, for different reasons: but I know of no one who chose to go to war to enhance his popularity.† Three years passed and the war in Iraq turned unpopular. Yet the Democratic senators and congressmen and presidential aspirants have been afraid to seem insufficiently nationalist.‡ They proclaimed

---

*D. 11 October 2001. "92% approval of Bush. . . . Walpole about the Tories 260 years ago: 'Now they are ringing their bells. Soon they will be wringing their hands.'"

D. 11 February 2006. "The Cuban missile crisis, too, came about not because of the Russians' presence there (that was a consequence) but because Kennedy was planning to invade Cuba within a year or so. In the end Kennedy made a compromise (to his credit), something that Bush and his people would not and could not have done."

†One possible exception may be McKinley against Spain in 1898. Yet he is an exception within an exception. The war against Spain had become popular by 1898; but McKinley was swept into war; he did not choose it to enhance his prestige.

‡D. 6 June 2001. "The Left and Liberals are weak everywhere. They have economic programs, whereas nationalism is not a program: it fills emotional, sentimental, mental, and spiritual needs."

their concern with Our Troops there; they did not ask why those troops were there at all. They, and popular discontent with the war, argued against its enormous financial costs and against the much less than enormous amount of blood shed there by Our Troops. They blamed the Iraqi government while they said nothing about the perhaps one hundred thousand deaths of Iraqi people, their monstrous sufferings largely caused by the American invasion and presence in that unfortunate country—an absence of concern different from American generosity extended to other defeated peoples in the past.*

D. 28 May 2005. "Liberalism, as a vital political ideology, is dead, but the Democrats don't know that. They have been, and are, more conservative in foreign policy than are the Republicans. But (a) this does not even occur to them, (b) they cower in fear of not seeming nationalist enough. Sic transit causa rei publicae."

D. 19 April 2003. "The cowardice of the Democrats; like the German Social Democrats on 1 August 1914, or the Catholic Centre Party on 23 March 1933. Not exactly, but largely so."

*D. 11 February 2002. "Gladstone 1879 about Afghanistan: 'Remember the rights of the savage as we call him. Remember . . . his humble home, remember that the sanctity of life in the hill villages of Afghanistan among the winter snows, is as inviolable in the eyes of Almighty God as can be your own.' "

D. 14 February 2002. "*One* American killed in combat. Hundreds of Afghans by our 'friendly fire.' This refers to what 'Defense' Secretary Rumsfeld calls 'nothing but collateral damage.' I write about this a letter to The New York Times. They will not print it."

During the past quarter-century the persistence of American popular nationalism grew together with something more recent: with the militarization of popular imagination. That has been inseparable from the growth of the American imperial presidency. Republicans and "conservatives" proclaim their opposition to Big Government; but they are the most aggressive proponents of enormous military expenditures and institutions, as if "defense" were not part of "government."* A president's journey now, especially abroad, includes more than one thousand agents, officers, servants, the retinue of a superimperial progress, dwarfing what we know of the retinue of a Genghis Khan or that of Louis XIV.

"The president"—says Section 2 of Article II of the Constitution—"shall be commander in Chief of the Army and Navy of the United States, and of the militia of the several states, when called into the actual service of the United States." Thereafter that short paragraph lists other presidential powers that have nothing to do with military matters. The brevity of the mention of a commander in chief—it is less than a full sentence—suggests that the Founders did not attach overwhelming importance to that role. Thereafter presidents, including former generals, chose not to emphasize their military function during their presidential tenure, in accord with the American tradition of the primacy of civilian over military rule. Of their constitutional

*D. 8 February 2002. "The Democrats do not dare criticize Bush's 'Defense' budget. What they ought to say is that it is not for Defense but for Offense."

prerogatives they were of course aware. Lincoln would dismiss and appoint generals; Truman knew that he had the right to fire MacArthur. But none of the presidents who governed this country during its great wars kept insisting that they were commanders in chief—not Washington, not Lincoln, not Wilson, not Roosevelt. Until now.*

Around 1980 the militarization of the image of the presidency began—with Reagan, who had no record of military service, having spent World War II in Hollywood. There were his fervent, sentimental, and sometimes tearful expressions when meeting or speaking to American soldiers, sailors, airmen. There was, too, his easy and self-satisfied willingness to employ the armed forces of the United States in rapid and spectacular military operations against minuscule targets of "evil," against "enemies" such as Grenada, Nicaragua, Libya. The present Bush, too, enjoys immersing himself in the warm bath of jubilant approbation at large gatherings of selected soldiery.

When Ronald Reagan was given a salute by military personnel, he would return it, shooting his right hand up to his bare head, his happy smile suggesting that this was something he liked to do. This unseemly and unnecessary habit was adopted by Reagan's successors, including Clinton and especially George W. Bush, who steps off his plane and cocks a jaunty salute. This ges-

---

*D. 30 April 2003. "Bush, as early as 2001: 'It's great to be commander in chief of this nation.' "

ture is wrong. Such a salute has always required the wearing of a uniform. But there is more to this than a corruption of military manners. There is something puerile in the Reagan and Clinton and now Bush salute. It is the gesture of someone who likes playing soldier. It also represents an undue exaggeration of a president's military function. War is a serious matter: but like the boy-soldier salute, a sentimentalization of military matters is puerile. Television depictions of modern technological warfare, too, make it seem as if a military campaign were but a superb game, an International Super Bowl that Americans are bound to win—and with few or no human losses. ("We'll keep our fighting men and women out of harm's way"—a senseless phrase uttered by members of Clinton's government.)

This is something new in American history. When the Roman Republic gave way to empire, the new supreme ruler, Octavian (Augustus), chose to name himself not "rex," king, but "imperator," from which our words *emperor* and *empire* derive, even though its original meaning was more like commander in chief. Thereafter Roman emperors came to depend more and more on their military. History does not repeat itself, but some of its conditions do. Is this the destiny of the United States?*

I do not know. What I know is that, beyond military games-

---

*D. 21 February 2002. "It seems to me that this diary is more and more like Reck-Malleczewen's *Tagebuch eines Verzweifelten.* My literary career is such as I had never expected or perhaps even wanted. But I despair of this nation and of

manship, puerility is a dangerous thing. There are, alas, many institutions in this country now, ranging from education to entertainment, that contribute to it, and powerfully so. But the sustenance of puerility may be even worse than decadence.* (After all, decadence is chock full of dissolving maggots of maturity, of remnant memories that puerility does not possess.) A puerile presidency may be but one symptom of the devolution of this republic into a military superstate. Consider but one, again entirely new, development: the American government's hiring and empowering tens of thousands of "private" mercenary fighters, "security" forces unknown and unaccounted for by Congress, freed of the governance and discipline of traditional military authority. Or consider the accumulated and secret powers of the Central Intelligence Agency. It was founded in 1947–48 for the purpose of coordinating intelligence previously gathered by different departments of the American government. Soon it assumed the power to arrange, direct, and perform secret operations[†]

---

many of its people. I think that the 21st century will not be the American century, but that some giant and unprecedented catastrophe may smite this country, probably of its own making, and perpetrated by one or more of their own. (Example: I do not fear an Arab crashing into the Limerick nuclear towers, but an American in a state of sexual or ideological frenzy.)"

*D. 27 February 2002. "I read that many of the Enron subsidiaries, 'partnerships,' had names from *Star Wars:* 'Chewbacca,' 'Jedi,' . . . , etc. Telling this is."

†D. 10 September 2005. "The dark, very dark corners of American history. CIA operations now are more secret and horrid doings than 'intelligence.' Prob-

throughout the entire world (and above its skies), superseding the authority and functions of the Department of State, establishing its own secret bases and prison camps and other lawless activities abroad, largely unknown and unsupervised by the elected representatives of the American people.

"The sudden change from democracy," wrote the great Jakob Burckhardt 150 years ago, "will no longer result in the rule of an individual, but in the rule of a military corporation. And by it, methods will perhaps be used for which even the most terrible despot would not have the heart."*

■

Nationalism and militarism are popular sentiments. That does not minimize, it maximizes their importance, since the most powerful element in the history of a democracy is the accumula-

---

ably in 1963, too, when it seemed to me that this frenetic fool Oswald had been taken up by the CIA a few months before he shot Kennedy. With that shooting the CIA had nothing to do; but they were frightened by the prospect that Oswald, when arrested and interrogated, would spit out his once CIA connection. Hence getting that gangster Ruby to shoot him next day; and—perhaps—their getting rid of Ruby a year later. Am not sure about this but think it quite plausible."

*D. 17 October 2001. "War was a profession for a long time—until the mobilization of masses of nationals. Now getting to be a profession again."

D. 6 February 2006. "Much of war now: mass killings from a distance. Soldiers' heads full of video games: 'We zap them!' American warplanes now named 'Predators,' 'Raptors.'"

tion not of materials but of opinions and sentiments. But that condition, in America, is not simple. There is the split-mindedness of so many Americans. (Split-mindedness, not schizophrenia: not a vertical division between what is conscious and less conscious; rather, the tendency to profess contradictory values within the same mind.) Americans tend to believe not only that they are a Chosen People* but also that what is good for America is good for the world: Yet at the same time they are not much interested in the world outside the United States. Many Americans admire their military unreservedly, they are willing to pay taxes for it at any time; yet they are not eager to be drafted for military service. Something of a split-mindedness prevails about their—so-called—materialism, too. Americans think that matter and money are most important, and that money is what most people most want:† but there are many kinds of evidences suggesting that for many Americans what matters is less their possession of money than their reputation for being able to spend it. Americans may be the least materialistic people in the world: there is enough evidence to argue this. However—there is now a fairly new condition, which is the spiritualization of matter: the intrusion of mind into

*D. 25 August 2006. "God will always smite, or chastise, those who think that they are his Chosen People."

†D. 20 January 2007. "Wendell Berry: 'Rodents and rats live with the laws of supply and demand. Human beings live with the laws of justice and mercy.' Or: they should. How true."

matter, into the very structure of it.* The great and profound danger in America is not materialism but a false spiritualism running rampant.†

■

A historian cannot and must not predict what will happen: but he may at least essay what will not happen. Liberalism will not recover.‡ But the Gadarene rush of former liberals to the "conservative"—or, more precisely, to the nationalist—side, their ephemeral overweight in the American commerce of intellectual and political ideas and preferences, will not last long either. There is one great and grave fault in the thinking of American conservatives as well as of American liberals. This is their belief in (linear) Progress. The liberals', ever more strained, propa-

---

*One example: what has happened to money. A century ago money was physically solid: its paper certificates exchangeable for gold or silver at par value. Yet for decades now, our money or stocks or bonds are not even on paper or in our *actual* possessions. They are *potential* values, consisting of configurations of graphic dust recorded on disks or films, deposited in distant institutions somewhere else. This is explained as part and parcel of the Information Revolution. But the very word *information* is false. It is not *in-formation*. Its proper description is *the imaging of matter.*

†D. 8 July 2005. "What is 'ownership' now? What are 'assets'? People who are told and who think that they are owners are mere renters."

‡D. 18 April 2003. "Can democracy (as we at least have known it) survive the disappearance of liberalism? May be worth a book."

ganda for the extension of limitless human "freedoms," their clinging to the Darwinist categories of evolution and "progress," not only compromises but goes counter to their once noble protection and defense of human dignity. The conservatives' propagation of American power throughout the world and, above it, into space, their thoughtless belief in the endless benefits of technology, amounts to a denial of every conservative view of human nature and of its limits. Liberals adulate Science; conservatives adulate Technology.* No great difference there. Consider but the favorite "conservative," and "Christian" idea of what *they* call "creationism," their propagation of the phrase of Intelligent Design, that is: God as an "intelligent designer," as if He were a rocket scientist or a computer wizard. That most of our self-proclaimed Conservatives ignore—worse, they dismiss with contempt—the cause of conservatism is reason enough to deny their very designation of themselves as conservatives.[†]

And yet: for the first time more and more Americans, some of them perhaps not quite consciously but more and more so, have begun to question the myth of endless mechanical and beneficial

---

*Reagan 1982: America's "divine destiny" is to reaffirm "this nation's special calling." George W. Bush about "Progress," 2002: "America is the hope of all mankind." 2001: "America must fight the enemies of Progress."

[†]D. 19 May 2001. "Bush's Secretary of the Treasury: tax cuts will give more money to Americans 'to have bigger houses and bigger cars.' Vice-President Cheney: Conservation is no solution, the solution is to produce more and more 'energy.' These are our Conservatives."

"Progress." They are still not an organized or a political minority, but they are not insignificant. They are concerned—after all, it involves their very lives—with what happens to their country and with their government's management and material destruction of nature (for which *environment* is a weak and stuttering word). They are the true conservatives, because of their respect for traditions, because of their authentic sincerity, incarnating a deep and pure spiritualism. Men and women such as Dorothy Day. Wendell Berry. George Kennan. Two of them are dead now but their influence will live on. I know some such people. They enliven my more and more isolated existence with hope. Even in American academic life a scatteration of true conservative probity has been evident for some time now. Some of the best American historians, thinkers, teachers, researchers, writers may be found—yes, they *ought* to be found—in the oddest places of this vast country, in little-known places, small colleges and universities, rather than in the repositories of Harvard or Yale or Princeton.*

*D. 18 December 2000. "At night I read the last number of *The Catholic Historical Review* and I am heartened (in a melancholy way). The standards of this journal are better now than they were, say, forty years ago. . . . Most of its articles and reviews are written by professors in small and obscure and provincial colleges and universities. I should write at least a postcard to some of these struggling men and women to encourage them. Sursum corda."

D. 11 February 2001. "The young conservatives of isi in West Chester. Their minds are more independent than what their adversaries may think.

"Mine is an odd destiny," Alexander Hamilton wrote to Gouverneur Morris in 1803. "Every day proves to me more and more that this American world was not made for me." It was not made for me either. Hamilton and I: we were not born here. I also know something that he did not know: the American handicap of a state and its doctrine born in the middle of the so-called Enlightenment, in the middle of the five hundred years of the so-called Modern Age that is now largely gone.

Still, there are moments, minutes, hours, when I can be happy. Even here, even now. It could be worse.

■

It could be worse: but very good it is not.

There are dualities in every human being. One duality: my Hungarian-European and my Anglo-American selves. Readers, believe me: the first of these pairs may be *deeper* than the second, but it does not *dominate* the second. The American, Benjamin Franklin trumpeted, is a self-made man. Not more than a half-truth (and so many half-truths are worse than are lies). I am not

They recognize the shallowness of present 'conservative' politicians and publicists such as Novak or Buckley. Some of them are fairly well-read."

D. 19 May 2005. "Yesterday I went with Ann King to give a talk to the history club in St. Joseph's Prep. The young students gave me an excellent impression, especially Ann's son Leo. Intelligent, quiet, well-mannered, introspective, kind. These young American Catholics may be the salt of the earth."

a self-made American. I have not dismissed my ancestry. But I am not a Hungarian writer, though I still can and could be that. This is not a result of choosing a language for writing. It is a consequence of thinking. Writing is one result of thinking. Is thinking the result of feeling? Yes and no. Thinking involves a choice. Feeling may be the source of a choice but not its result. Ignore feeling. My mind is concerned with this, my adopted country, and with its history. It is, too, with my native country and with its history. Sometimes less. Seldom more.

When, on rare and memorable occasions, I was called a master of my native language, my mind was atremble with sentiments of gratitude. When, on other rare and memorable occasions, I was called a master of English prose, I was proud beyond reason. In the introduction of my perhaps most extraordinary book, *A Thread of Years*, I wrote: "In the second part of each annualized chapterette, I challenge myself. *Myself:* because my interlocutor is my alter ego. He is not an imaginary person; he is not a composite or a confection of someone else. He is more commonsensical, more pragmatic, more direct, more down-to-earth than is the narrator of the vignette, and we argue, add, subtract, agree, disagree. . . . When the idea (or, rather, the plan) of such a construction first occurred to me I cannot tell. It may be that while the author of my vignettes and their occasional defendant is my European self, my challenger and debater is my American one. It may be: perhaps not. But it is no use to discuss this further."

I wrote half of my more than two dozen books during the past twenty years of my life. Their writing took me (and still takes me) about two years on the average. A "prolific" writer, people on occasion write or say.* I dislike that adjective. It is not a pretty one. In the *Oxford English Dictionary* it has not one pejorative meaning: still, I dislike it. That does not matter. What does matter is my alienation from my profession. Fourteen years ago, when I was made to resign (because of age) from teaching at my college, the then chairman of the history department of the University of Pennsylvania asked me to teach there a single course in a single semester that I took up with pleasure. I did this for three years. That history department consisted of forty-five professors, of whom I knew two. Soon it was obvious that none of the others desired to meet me. In my third and last semester I had memorable students, six of them, the seventh a faker. They surprised me with a gift of a bottle of fine French champagne on the last day of class. A few days later my wife brought me the telephone. I was in the garden, mowing. The new chairman of the department spoke haltingly, in an unsteady voice: she said that

---

*D. 29 April 2003. "People ask me how much fun it is to write. No, I say: the fun is not writing, that is work, the fun (if it is fun at all) is having written. It occurs to me that this is the v. opposite of sex. (A good aphorism perhaps, but not really true in every instance, esp. not for women. The 'finish' in lovemaking means much to me, as in the case of fine wine.")

they had no place for me any longer. Of course I was disappointed: but disappointments so often turn out to be blessings.
Now I had even more time and air and space for writing. A year
or two later, a friend, a historian far away, rang me up to chat. He
asked me how I was doing. A sudden thought, or a turn of phrase,
sprang in my mind. "I have many things to complain about," I
said, "but I have no reason to complain."*

Through fifty years of college teaching and writing, often I
have run into ignorance, disdain, exclusion, professional snob-
bery, gray ice on other professors' faces! Professional academics
are a kind of guild. Why should they not be uneasy with this
strange presence in their guild? I have come from the outside as a
very young man from a distant, small country in Europe, with
academic credentials not entirely identical or even similar to the
American Ph.D.; I got a job and stayed on teaching in a small
Catholic college of no unusual distinction. I thought that I would
try to make my name known not dependent on the customary
academic stepladder, that slippery and wooden *gradus ad Parnas-
sum*, but by writing remarkable books. What books? Books on
various subjects interesting for me, at times against the accepted

*D. 6 December 2006. Goethe: "Was man in der Jugend begehrt hat, hat
man im Alter die Fülle. [What one wished for when young one gets a fill when
one is old.] Wise and true—in most circumstances, without people being much
aware of it. But 'Fülle' [fulfillment?] in old age is hardly more than contentment. Gissing: 'Contentment so often means resignation, abandonment of the
hope seen to be forbidden.' That too is not *always* so. Acceptance: yes."

ideas and categories of their current specialists.* Worse: as time went on, I attacked some of them; indeed, I attacked my very profession. I argued and wrote that history was, and is, not a Science: that often the "professional" category applied to historianship was imprecise; that so many academic historians were not even interested in history very much; what they were interested in was their historianship, their status within "the profession"—and not that "history" consists of and depends on words, without which "facts" have no meaning. Why, then, should I have expected the sympathy, let alone the embrace, of the guild?[†] Was I entitled to have my cake and eat it too? No. I remain aware of the pettiness, of the shortsightedness of professional academics. But *comprendre, c'est pardonner:* I respect and appreciate and, whenever I can, support those younger men and women struggling to enter the guild—if *guild* remains a proper word at all.

Once, about fifteen or so years ago, I overheard another professor talking about me: "He is a historian; but he is really a writer." (He said this with a slightly deprecatory tone; he did not

---

*Do not think that I am against specialists. To the contrary: I respect them; and I am saddened by their gradual disappearance. They have *loved* their subjects, after all. For the specialist described in the hoary nineteenth-century adage as someone who knows more and more about less and less is, alas, a rare bird nowadays. Instead, we have Experts who know less and less about more and more.

[†]D. 1 February 2005. ". . . in the words and thoughts of even those who hate or dislike us there is always at least a small crumb of reality."

know that I was standing within hearing distance of him.) I think I was—and I still am—amused, not wounded. Yes, I am a writer; and a historian who cannot write well enough cannot be a good historian. We have, and should have, no jargon. Our instrument is the common language. We write and teach and speak and think with words.

■

Around me, within thirty or forty miles, are at least five universities and dozens of colleges, staffed by tens of thousands of academic intellectuals. I know few of them. I have lived around here for more than sixty years; in this very place for fifty-four. There is one difference from what still existed, say, one generation ago. Then there were in my neighborhood some men and women who were not academics but were then called "intellectuals": people who bought and read books and periodicals, who had interests in art, who took some comfort or pride in their broadmindedness. A class of opinion, rather than of society, they were. *Intellectual*, as a noun, appeared in the English language, in Britain and then in the United States, in the 1880s and 1890s. It was, oddly, an immigrant noun, a word and usage from Tsarist Russia, where intellectuals, no matter how few, were more or less recognizable men and women. I had not come from such a world: for a long time, through many decades, I bridled against being called An Intellectual: I found that many of the minds of such people were more narrow than they had thought themselves, or so broad as to be flat; I declared that I was a teacher and a writer and that was that. But during the past twenty or thirty years there came a change. Intellectuals in America, as a social class of opinion, have just about ceased to exist. There are a few intellectuals among academics, but of course there are many more academics who are not intellectual at all. I would have never thought that one day I should miss the presence of intellectuals around me; I do—a little—now.

The world of universities and of intellectual commerce at large is now more remote from me than it was before. But the subject of this book, and perhaps especially of this chapter, is not I but the world around me. And there great changes, transformations, have occurred. One of them is not wholly new. It began at least one hundred years ago. It is the decline of the written and of the printed word: the change from a verbal to a pictorial "culture": indeed, to the ways of thinking and seeing: the rising appearance of a new Middle or, rather, Dark Ages of symbols, pictures, images, abstractions. This has happened together with a breakdown of normal communications—in spite, or rather, because of the propaganda of an Information Age.*

*D. 8 February 2001. "I finish Dava Sobel's truly excellent *Galileo* book. I did not know that Milton and Hobbes and Elsevir took the trouble to visit Galileo around 1640, two or three years, before he died. This is amazing, this kind of communication among interested people (Milton and Hobbes were not astronomers or scholars, Elsevir a Dutch printer & publisher). They did not flit to Florence in 90 minutes from Heathrow or Amsterdam but they braved the—

And beneath and beyond these phenomena runs the tide of cynicism. For a long time many Americans, idealists as well as pragmatists, were optimistic about democracy, overestimating the potential intelligence of their people. But even an illusory idealism is preferable to a calculating cynicism. During the twentieth century the purveyors of education and of information and of entertainment, the managers of intellectual and artistic commerce, the publishers of printed matter, the manipulators of visual matter and, worst of all, the administrators of American education, have established and solidified their careers and fortunes through a, to them "practical" but in reality cynical, un-

---

then feared and dangerous—passage of the Alps, among other dreadful wear & tear of traveling in those days. This too gives the lie to Modern Communications. Galileo was not a Nobel Prize winner, he was not a celebrity, he did not attend conferences, etc. Yet they knew about him and desired to meet him. There are academics and scholars, within thirty miles from here, dozens of them, now who have never even looked at books that I had written in their 'field,' about their 'subjects.' I am not writing this to complain, but to put down what I think of the Information Age and the Communications Revolution— worse than misnomers. Again: the trouble is not with people's inability to think but with their unwillingness to think—i.e., lack of imagination, lack of curiosity. (Four hundred years ago a 'curieux,' in French, meant an intellectual.) I had noticed the same phenomenon reading the correspondence of Vico, who was even less of a Celebrity than Galileo, who taught in Naples, which at the time was a fairly backward university: yet people in faraway France knew about him and corresponded with him."

derestimation of the potential intelligence of the American people, very much including their youth. There are myriad examples of this.

Readers of books: they still exist, scattered in some of the oddest nooks and crannies of this large country. But the breakdown of communications has affected them too. One of the outcomes of that is the rapid deterioration of attention, the nervous constriction of its span.* This includes academics and scholars. So many of them no longer buy books. Or even read them: they prefer to read, instead, reviews. Those too, they read fast, since their interest is seldom in the matter discussed: it is what "A" ventures, or dares, to say about "B."

It could be worse. This is a very big country. Not everywhere, and not always, does its cult of equality—constraining as it often is—imprison us into uniformity. Solitude and inattention are not everywhere, and not always destructive. By and large they have allowed (rather than permitted) me to invent my own occupation, my maverick profession and career, writing different books,

---

*Including myself. At noon every weekday, I walk out to my mailbox on the road. As I gather the accumulation of mail, my heart sinks as I clutch (not without difficulty) the journals and magazines sent to me, to many of which I do not subscribe, and to the daily *New York Times* to which I do. Sometimes the Saturday delivery of the latter is thickened with the supplements of the Sunday edition: an extra three pounds of paper to carry, but the physical burden of which is nothing compared to the sinking feeling they bring to my mind.

each of them published by reputable firms, some of them reviewed here and there with some respect. What is much more important: they are noted by a scattering of readers, many of them young, some of them true "conservatives." My occasional encounters with them give me much pleasure. So, constrained but not entirely disallowed I am, by what has been "developing" around me.

■

In the same place, on the same piece of land, I have been living for fifty-four years now. This alone makes me different from my neighbors. I hardly know my closest neighbors now, nothing of their lives, of their characters, of their minds. We are parcels of different, increasingly different, worlds. The civilization to which I belonged, whose child I was, which I tried to prize and protect and reconstruct within this house, on these few acres, in this countryside, in this Pennsylvania, in these United States, in this world, has largely vanished. The last people who belonged to it, whom I knew, who were dear to me, have vanished too. I am a remnant, with less pride and more misery in my heart, by much what I hear and see. People with whom one would talk about some things, in a certain language, exist no more. It is not like those French aristocrats who fled after 1790 and then talked about life before 1789, the ancien régime: a few years later most of those men and women returned to their ancestral places. Now I think that I am the only one around me who has lived in the same place for fifty-four years. That circumstance may have earned me some respect, from some. But, by and large, it contributes to most of my new neighbors' sense of my un-Americanness. Pennsylvania is among the more sedate states of the Union. Its population has hardly increased and the average age is older than elsewhere. Yet the average Pennsylvanian now moves every four or five years. His mind depends on an abstract outside world. With his television and computer and Internet and two automobiles and at least two mobile telephones, he is connected to a world, to his American world, more than ever before. These things render him different from his restless ancestors. Americans have always been restless. But not like they are now, moving from suburb to suburb.

Human nature does not change. Human character does not much change either. But it is malleable. What changes is human behavior, because of thinking: or, rather, because of acquired habits of thinking. I wrote umpteen times that people do not *have* ideas, they *choose* them. To this let me add that, almost always, people will adjust their ideas to circumstances, rather than adjust circumstances to their ideas. Circumstances are what I am thinking and writing about. Some of these circumstances being that I know little or nothing about my close neighbors now, and they know little or nothing about me. I would not mind knowing a little more about them, but this is not reciprocal. I do not know what goes on and very little of what exists inside their houses.

They do not know, or wish to know, what goes on in mine. My interest in them may be larger than theirs in me, but that is not the point. They know very little about their other neighbors too. This is the world that now exists around me.

Thirty years ago about six thousand people lived in my township. I knew the names of perhaps half of them. Not now.

I know that I can depend on one, perhaps two, of my close neighbors in an emergency, in the good old American way, for help. That, too, could be worse. Still, most of them, married couples, are away for most of the day, even on weekends. That circumstance—or call it a condition—knocks away the foundation of the American suburban aspirations of forty or fifty years ago. Those had a sentimental foundation, but then that is so with all that seem (but only seem) to be materialist aspirations in America. It was the ideal of a house, one's own, on a small grassy plot, away from a packed city and its crowded traffic, a sunny life, with new neighbors and friends, close but not separated from each other by high fences and walls: an ideal for a woman even more than for a man (the latter having to learn some lawn work and carpentry). Very soon it did not turn out that way. American womanhood in the suburbs turned out to be lonely, in many ways lonelier than the lives of pioneer wives in the middle of empty prairies in a sod house. Sooner or later, every young wife in the suburbs decided to go out somewhere, to be "employed," to "work" (as if keeping a house, feeding and caring for a family, were not work).* More than two hundred years ago Samuel Johnson was—and now remains, as almost always—right. "To be happy at home is the end of all human endeavor." To be happy outside the home is now the aim of much American endeavor—certainly for the young, and for not so young "adults" too.

Sweeping generalizations these are: but then generalizations, like brooms, ought to sweep . . . We had friends, most of them old Americans, not academics, not intellectuals, but men and women who read a little, traveled a little, cultivated their gardens (not a little), with whom I and my wife could talk about houses and gardens and places and people and things, with our common—not identical, but common—sensibilities. Many of them had what Goethe once called "die Höflichkeit des Herzens," the courtesies of the heart. Then they began to die, they went away and died. Thirty years ago we had dinner parties in their houses or in ours. Now we have friends for dinner once or twice a year. Family dinners of course more often. This, too, could be worse.

One more example of the breakdown of communications: my—our—everyone's—divorce, distance, separation from Phila-

---

*As the so-called Industrial Revolution grew to completion, about 130 years ago, for the first time a working man could afford to keep his wife at home. She needed not work outside of it. That lasted, by and large, for less than a century. (As did the Industrial Revolution. In 1874 in England, around 1910 in the United States for the first time, more people were employed in industry than in agriculture. By 1960 in the United States more people were employed in administration and in services than in industrial and agricultural work together.)

delphia. More than a half-century ago I and my wife chose to live in Chester County: still, we were Philadelphians. The movement of the middle classes to the suburbs had begun, but a sense of Philadelphianness prevailed. Those who lived beyond the city traveled there each weekday to work, as did my first wife then. We, and many others, were drawn to the city because of its stores, shops, institutions, theaters, the orchestra. Much of Philadelphia I loved. A quarter of a century later I wrote a book about Philadelphia, *Philadelphia, Patricians and Philistines, 1900–1950* (1981). But Philadelphia is a faraway, a foreign city now. Faraway: because of the very "progress"—that is: the partial collapse of communications, and of physical transportation. The godawful Schuylkill Expressway, built in the 1950s, was constructed to bring suburbs and city closer and closer together. The very opposite happened. Soon it made normal driving into the city difficult; and thereafter nearly impossible, impacted as it is almost every hour of the day and night. Foreign too: no one I know works in the city any longer. No one I know does Christmas shopping in Philadelphia. No one I know subscribes to the Orchestra.* I know but one friend who lives in the city. I no

---

*The Academy of Music for the Orchestra is gone. The Orchestra now performs in the Kimmel Center, an enormous crimson-painted, airport-like hangar. Sixteen years ago I was in a pastry shop in Helsinki, Finland, full of women and old ladies talking and sipping coffee or tea, before the concert of the Helsinki Philharmonic. What a bourgeois scene in the midst of so-called socialist welfare-state Scandinavia! I felt a sense of permanence, a sense that,

longer rate a Philadelphia telephone directory: if I need a number there, I have to call Information. There is a monthly magazine, *Philadelphia*, of thirty years' standing now. "Standing"—or rather, lying in dentists' offices. When I pick it up I recognize not one person and not one place in it. It might as well be a magazine of Atlanta or Seattle or Dallas. The city of Philadelphia has become alien.*

■

True nostalgia is a desire less for a time than for a place. True patriotism is a love for one's country and for its traditions. Philadelphia did not have much of a literary tradition, but it had considerable and even great painters, from Peale to Eakins. But there was a group of eastern Pennsylvania, not Philadelphia, painters and paintings—what and how they painted, the small world that they reflected and represented widens my tired old

---

say, thirty years later the same kind of people, the same kind of orchestra, the same kind of city life would prevail—when the Philadelphia Orchestra would be performing (if at all) in the King of Prussia Mall.

*D. 28 April 2006. "Yesterday I drove into Philadelphia, for a radio interview. . . . I got in early, walked over to Rittenhouse Square, which was full of people and still nice. Around me a Philadelphia that I remember but no longer know. The McIlhenny house, "1914," shut down, its windows sightless, with a gray protective film covering them. The Barclay bar, where I had so many memories, now must be entered through a door from the street; it is a kind of grill-room."

eyes and clutches my heart. They are, loosely called, the Pennsylvania Impressionists. Around 1900–1910 they began to gather, they chose to settle, live, and work in what was then still an entirely rural landscape on the shore and in the mild valleys of the Delaware, in eastern Bucks County, Pennsylvania. Among them were Redfield, Garber, Lothrop, Folinsbee, Baum, Leith-Ross, Coppedge, Meltzer, Schofield, Rosen, Spencer, Taylor, Van Roekens, Witherspoon. Two were women; two of them Englishmen: for whatever reason, they chose to live here. Others had come here from the flat American Midwest. Was theirs an "Artists' Colony"? Yes and no. They had nothing in common with the intellectual self-consciousness, with the self-proclaimed radicalism of the Provincetown Cape Cod people circa 1913 (often referred in American intellectual or art history as "the Little Renaissance"—well, it was very little indeed). Most of them, with their gnarled hands, were master woodworkers and carpenters too, craftsmen able to build houses and barns. After they lifted their nimble fingers from their brushes, their eyes moved from the exquisite nuances of their palettes and colors to the straight, hard, precise fitting of grooves and planks and boards. Around 1910 Edward Redfield wrote that "Bucks County was a place where an independent, self-sufficient man could make a living from the land, bring up a family and still have the freedom to paint as he saw fit." How admirable! How American! In a once country. At a once time.

Yes, they were Impressionists, but not simply American imita-

tors or successors of the famous great French painters before
them. They had one thing in common with these French mas-
ters, or with other Impressionists all over the world. It was a new
way of painting because of a new comprehension of seeing (a
comprehension rather than a conscious knowledge; Pascal: "We
understand more than we know"), an understanding of the limitations of the human mind and eye that might actually enrich the
capacity, the depth, and the beauty of human vision. Or, in other
words: a participation* in the world one sees. Whence their sug-
gestive rendering of the colors and waters and seasons and air, of
the farmhouses and barns and trees and paths and hillsides
around Cuttaloosa or New Hope or Lumberville. Some of their
paintings are ineffably beautiful. I am not a critic of art, not even

---

*D. 28 December 2006. "Impressionism tells, or should tell us, in retro-
spect, that it is *participation.* The 'reality' is not outside but what the painter
sees: whence what he can suggest. Of course these painters did not know the
historic meaning of this. But their impressionism thus preceded quantum
physics by about a half-century. (Of course: the artist is the antenna of the race
—or, rather, of civilization.) After that: cubism, abstract art, etc.—and string
theory in physics."

D. 16 August 2006. "Impressionism: the great recognition, of course not
only of plein-air, but that the world outside us is inseparable from what we see,
from what comes from inside us, whence we must illustrate ('lustrate,' in the
original sense of that word) what and how we see. Thus 'Impressionism' was
not a symptom of decadence but a surge of consciousness. . . . The degeneration after it was awful but it will not last."

of their art. My subject is not their method or even their accomplishment. It is their superb and modest present of a world, of an American world that is now gone, a portion of a world with its provincialness and plenitude, including plenty of modest decency and goodness,* of landscapes, God- *and* man-made. A landscape is not wholly "nature," it is God-made but with signs of a human presence. There were no paintings of landscapes in the Middle Ages. We have come to see the beauty of our world differently now.

They lived in the country, in a small portion of the Pennsylvania American country. They were among the last incarnations of a civilization that had begun to sink in their lifetime, at the end of the Bourgeois Age, and of the American bourgeois interlude. They would be surprised to be called "bourgeois," which was a curse word employed not only by revolutionaries but by intellectuals and artists during more than one hundred years; but they were bohemians not at all. Well, their beautiful small world was going, too, together with them. Around 1935 Bucks County and

---

*Lathrop: "The finest art, the finest in life, is formed by love." (He disappeared, drowned while repairing his boat on the New England coast during the September 1938 hurricane.) Garber: "I am a very happy man. I am a simple man. . . . I am enthusiastic about my painting. I have few theories about it. . . . I had a wonderful life." (He died at the age of seventy-eight. He had fallen off a ladder.) He "would lovingly touch a small blossom from his garden and growl at his daughter: 'You only have to look at a flower to know there's a God!' " (from the reminiscences of his daughter).

New Hope were discovered by the New York theatrical and in-tellectual aggregation. Soon afterward most of the painters were dead and gone. And yet—about sixty years later their heritage survived the noisy, fretful, self-consciously cynical world of the-ater directors and their writers. The bucket of art criticism may be a pit of snakes; and yet the Pennsylvania Impressionists are beginning to be rediscovered. So it could be, it could have been worse. As for me: it is to the provincial world they reflected and represented to which my heart belongs.

■

More than two hundred years ago, Edmund Burke wrote in his *Reflections on the Revolution in France:*

> To be attached to the subdivision, to love the little platoon we belong to in society, is the first principle (the germ as it were) of public affections. It is the first link in the series by which we proceed towards a love to our country and to mankind.

A few years ago Wendell Berry wrote:

> My devotion thins as it widens. I care more for my house-hold than for the town of Port Royal, more for the town of Port Royal than for the County of Henry, more for the County of Henry than for the State of Kentucky, more for the State of Kentucky than for the United States of Amer-

ica. But I do not care more for the United States of America than for the world.

I care more for my household than for Schuylkill Township, more for Schuylkill Township than for Chester County, more for Chester County than for the State of Pennsylvania, more for the State of Pennsylvania than for the United States of America, and I do not care more for the United States of America than for the world: at least for the world of what remains of Western civilization.

■

I chose to live in Chester County, in the countryside. Now the suburbs have come close. Until five or six years ago there were no houses closer than one thousand feet from me. Now there are. It makes no sense for me to bewail that. This has happened to millions of other people, Americans.

I still live on three acres that belonged to my first wife's ancestors for almost two hundred and fifty years. After 1955 those other 136 acres to my east, with some old buildings, were no longer of her family. They were largely unchanged by a new owner and his second wife and their children who inherited it but did not live there. Ten years ago they sold it to large developers. Now there are new more-than-one- or two-million-dollar houses, three of them now less than a thousand feet from us, visible in the winter. But it could have been worse. I was able, as an official of the township,* to advise and convince the owners not to challenge the township zoning ordinance: I told them that that would cost them many years and much money. Whence I have now three new neighbors, not thirty.

A few years after 1955, on winter evenings, I read through, arranged, preserved, some of my wife's ancestors' papers. I also cared for the family cemetery. One of my wife's few prominent ancestors had established a family cemetery a mile to the east from here. The first family graves there go back to the eighteenth century. The last family member buried there was my father-in-law in 1955; I drew his gravestone to resemble some of the other old ones. Later I became one of the trustees of the Anderson Burial Ground. There were no wreaths, no visitors. The gate was broken and the stone wall cracked. The upkeep cost some work and money. One of the trustees died. Eventually I remained the one in charge. I did not do much.

It could have been worse. About eight years ago I convinced the Supervisors of the Township to take over the cemetery,

---

*D. 20 December 2000. "Tonight the monthly Planning Commission meeting. Blessedly short. (It is very cold tonight.) After the agenda a little superficial banter. . . . Not about essentials: we (they) are more and more dependent on the technical statements of engineers and other experts, whereby essentials are obscured and often not dealt with. This is not democracy at best. But it is also not American democracy at its worst."

assuring its perpetual upkeep.* Repairs were made, a historical plaque was installed, on which are embossed the names and dates (I had been able to reconstruct them) of twenty-one of the twenty-two men and women and children buried there through two hundred years. On 4 November 2006 there was a ceremony. The plaque, handsomely made, was dedicated. The day commemorated, too, the founding of Schuylkill Township 180 years before, its separation from Charlestown Township promoted by Isaac Anderson then. I was named the first Distinguished Citizen of Schuylkill Township. A resolution honoring me by the Pennsylvania House of Representatives was handed to me. It was a very American ceremony, with an American willingness of the heart. I embraced Norman and Ted, two of the township supervisors, my old friends.

■

About ten years ago, at the very end of *A Thread of Years*, I wrote: "It's all over for this work, for this book" (which ended with the

---

*D. 19 December 2000. "Yesterday I go to the Orphans' Court in West Chester with Ted Ryan and our township attorney for the judge to approve the transfer of the ownership of the Anderson Burial Ground to the township. This is the end of a more than four-year-old process. It goes well and swiftly and I am mildly impressed by the respectful demeanor of the people in the courtroom when Judge Wood comes in."

year 1969, which I saw as a milestone marking the end of Anglo-American civilization),

and probably for most of the world that I (and you, my alter ego) cherish and stick to, but God is infinitely good, since it is He and not Voltaire who allows and even prods us to cultivate our garden. And what a beautiful afternoon it is! Look at the color of the water. And at Stephanie's yellow and blue flowers. That heap of pots there is her job, but there are the heads of my asparagus appearing and the raspberries are coming out. Let's try to coax her out of the kitchen and busy ourselves there. What a beautiful afternoon this is!

Ten years later Stephanie is dead and the asparagus and the raspberries do poorly, if at all. But there is Pamela's beauteous mass of yellow and red flowers. Our terrace, our garden, our house is an island in the midst of an encroaching tide of suburbs and cement.* But there is another island, too: a real one, out in the stream, ever more in our sight, growing month by month.

*And now our three acres have become an animal refuge, too, for many animals who were driven out of their habitats by the "developments" around us. Besides the habitual squirrels and rabbits and groundhogs we have a herd of deer, two foxes (last winter a coyote), in the air and in the stream all kinds of birds and waterfowl, including herons and a white egret and an occasional stately swan, and a bald eagle appearing once in a while.

What was only a few years ago a large placid shallow lake is filling up, with silt, from "developments," more and more of them, upstream. Man-made, irremovable, incorrigible. In a few years our once lake will become a stream narrowing each winter, each year.

Still there is that forest of greenery on the other side of the water; and on this side, our grass descends to it, emerald and gilt under the sun, spinach-green after the shadows advance across it. One now unforgettable evening, about a dozen years ago, I suddenly decided to row down to my friends, the Reeves, two miles away. So I went, with the plashing of my oars the only sound, except for one far cry of a loon. I rowed into their inlet and clambered up on their steep overgrown slope. We had a drink. I started to row homeward. I was alone, in the middle of the reservoir. Soon I saw not a single light. Alone, on that dark indigo water, as if one hundred miles away from any town, out in some wilderness, under a sickle moon. I was full of gratitude for what God and this country had allowed me, for this silent world where I belonged, where I had chosen to live. A mile ahead, after the bend, I saw the lights of our house. In twenty minutes I was home.

■

Another night, eight years into the twenty-first century, another night falls now, after another day. The twilight of senility falls on my mind. Ahead of me, attracting me to the blissful solitude of sleep, that island within islands. Strange islands my dreams are!* I sleep eight, nine hours every night. When I wake up my dreams surround me, like clouds weighing down. They have to disperse before I face the new day—which, at my age, is no longer "le viergé, le vivace, le bel aujourd'hui." There are no dreams without thinking. There is no thinking without memories. We can have no memories, no dreams of the future, of any future.

Old age is a shipwreck.† It could be worse. I am alone: but not alone. One day or one night I will die. But remembered I shall be, by my wife, by my children, by my grandchild, by my step-children, by my remaining friends, by my platoon.‡

---

*D. 28 February 2001. " . . . *nothing* ever occurs in our dreams that we had not experienced or thought or dreamt about before. 'We live forward but we can only think backward' is as applicable to dreams as to thinking awake. Only the associations are more varied ones. In sum: when we dream we do not really think differently, we only remember differently."

†D. 13 August 2001. "[Said] De Gaulle. For some people. For me: a leaking ship."

‡My platoon includes my carpenter, my housepainter, my plumber, my electrician. We have known each other, we have respected each other, we have depended on each other for many decades now. The president of my bank, the superintendent of my local school district (giant building less than one mile from me demanding more than half of ten thousand dollars from me each year), my representative in the Congress of the United States, I do not know them and they know me not.

■

One last summary chart of my itinerary. What a strange life I have had, what a strange solitary ship, what a strange ship, what strange seas! When I was young, did I, could I imagine that I'd live this long? Well, whatever my genes, my life in America made this possible for me. Had I remained in Hungary I would not now be alive. I left my country when I was young, at the age of twenty-two,* because I set my sight to the west, The West. I thought that the victory of America, of Britain, of the "West," meant restoration as much as progress: a restoration of the conservative and liberal freedoms and institutions that Hitler and the Germans and others had been ready to raze. Decline of The West, some day: but still a long sunny afternoon of human freedom and human dignity, perhaps even for many decades, during which because of their barbaric stupidities Russia's empire and Communism will not last. I was right about the latter but that was about all. Soon I recognized—more, I became ever more deeply, ever more painfully aware—of what separated and still separates me from almost? perhaps all Americans I know. This is

*D. 18 January 2005. "Sixty years ago today, 18 Jan. '45, 9:45 A.M. Budapest, the first Russians. It was something else than 'liberation,' it was Zero Hour. From then on, Russia and America. And now only America, with dwarves ruling it, and the world. I knew what the Russians meant, and I went, fled to America, for an older, more decent, freer life in a free country, in a free world. So much of that now . . . gone."

my awareness that I—we—have now lived not only in the twilight but beyond the end of an entire great historical epoch, of the great European and bourgeois age of about five hundred years, of which the establishing of the United States of America was an inexorable part.* That kind of knowledge behooves me, a historian. But it is also engraved in my heart.

There is no eternal return in history. It is not like a pendulum that swings back. There are not even ephemeral returns. Some inclinations do reappear, in circumstances that are new. There always has been a strain in the American mind that is older than the Enlightenment, that was (and is) contrary to the Enlightenment. I have called it the medieval strain in America: the particularly American split-minded coexistence of medieval with supermodern habits of mind.† Seven or eight hundred years ago the medieval world was incapable to face the condition that contradictory matters could coexist within the same accepted doctrines or dogmas. Johan Huizinga, great historian, wrote in *The Passing*

---

*D. 9 May 2002. "Most Americans have no sense or vision that the entire so-called Modern Age is over. Europeans uneasily sense this but have no longer any vigor to resist it."

†One example. In 1705 the city fathers of Philadelphia outlawed fornication, which was a rather medieval thing to do, and added the clause that the innocent spouses of the guilty parties had the right to sue for divorce, which was very modern, very American.

D. 8 March 2001. "Near Pasadena we drive by a fundamentalist church with a sign outside: 'Dieting for Jesus.'"

of the Middle Ages: "A too systematic idealism gives a certain rigidity of the conception of the world. . . . Men disregarded the individual qualities and the fine distinctions of things, deliberately and of set purpose, in order always to bring them under some general principle. . . . What is important is the impersonal. The mind is not in search of individual realities, but of models, examples, norms. . . . There is in the Middle Ages a tendency to ascribe a sort of substantiality to abstract concepts." All of this was and is as true of Puritans as it is of Disneyland, of Superman as of the public relations man, of most American Fundamentalists and Evangelicals as of many American Catholics,* of television as of the American War against Evil. Around us are now symptoms, signs of a new Dark Ages—except that history does not really repeat itself.

That is, too—and this goes beyond America—why the deep crisis of Christianity and perhaps especially of the Roman Catholic Church,† is not soluble through a return to medievalism, or to the Old Mass, or to new catechisms—no matter how the new medieval habits of mind with their powerful but superficial

---

*D. 28 January 2001. "I go to Mass and walk out, during the sermon. The pastor speaks of angels and saints in Heaven watching the Superbowl."

D. 26 June 2005. "Didn't go to church and didn't get the Sunday *New York Times.* Relieved by neglecting the latter but not the former."

†D. 22 April 2007. "We are living through the spiritualization of matter. That is much of what Catholicism is about: but now, with abstraction rising everywhere, what will the Church do with that?"

sureties, may again attract masses of the faithful. The Church, my church, must now reconcile itself to be a church of a minority of the truly believing*—as it was, of course, in entirely different circumstances and with entirely different prospects after the age of the catacombs eighteen hundred or so years ago. The Church must remain a single, lonely lighthouse of human comprehension, of wisdom, a proponent of love. For God's (and their own) sake, Christians must steel themselves against temptations of popularity and success, against actors who may become Anti-Christs, kissing babies, blessing believers, announcing that they are great champions of prosperity and heroic warriors against evil. Such thoughts have often led me to think about the great division at the second coming of Christ, at the end of the world— when Christians will be divided into a large conformist majority and a pitiful, suffering, and believing minority, just as were Jews so divided two thousand years ago, at the first coming of Christ.† That does not belong here. What may belong here is the de-

---

*D. 15 July 2007. "Went to Mass, and took Communion. The Gospel was about the Good Samaritan. The priest's sermon was deeply felt, honest. . . . St. Mary's has now been half-empty, few young people. I do *not* mind being among a churchgoing people who are a minority. I know this is wrong, but at least I think that this is not because I am a snob, it is because of my distrust and even fear of crowds, including energetic crowds of believers."

†D. 20 January 2002. "The Vatican declared a very fine thing, that Jews and Christians belong *together* in expecting the Messiah except of course that the former did not recognize His first coming. A good-hearted and wise gesture to Jews."

spondent cry of a deep-thinking contemporary of ours, the Russian Tatyana Tolstoya, perhaps particularly relevant to the recovering Russian Orthodox now, but alas, too, of so many in the West: "We have no faith: we're afraid to believe, because we're afraid that we'll be deceived." I think that I am not afraid to believe—perhaps because I am a gambler.

FOUR

The World Behind Me:
My Native Country

In this book, *Last Rites*, I am loath to refer back to its predecessor, *Confessions of an Original Sinner*, but now—especially in this chapter—this I can hardly avoid. I finished the writing of *Confessions* in 1989, at the age of sixty-five. That time for writing such an autobiographical book was just about right. So were, too, its proportions. One-third of it, three of its nine chapters, dealt with one-third of my life, about twenty-two of my then sixty-five years, in my native country, Hungary—the following two-thirds, about forty-three years, with myself in the United States. Now another twenty years have passed. The years of my childhood and of my youth have now dwindled to hardly more than one-fourth of my entire life. However—in that very year, 1989, something else happened, leading to an important change in my relationship to my native country. In 1989 the Communist regime and the Russian occupation of Hungary came to their end. It was also the end of the cold war—indeed, of the entire historical twentieth century, 1914 to 1989, of the century of two world wars and the cold war which was but a consequence of the second. That much I knew right then and there. How all of that would affect my life I did not know.*

I thought not much about that. Like many millions of predecessors, I was an immigrant to the United States in 1946, but perhaps not—well, at least not a typical—émigré or refugee. There were reasons for that condition, including some particularly my own. I had fled a Hungary that fell into the Soviet sphere and that was about to be ruled by Communists. When I arrived in the United States I knew that there was no real prospect for me to return to my native country within a foreseeable future; I thought that it would remain under the Russian thumb for a long time. Moreover: my professional ambitions, in-

---

*In December 1989, in a circular questionnaire, "A Brush with History" in *American Heritage*, I wrote "Enough for One Life! I lived through the Second World War in the middle of Europe. I saw the fiery retreat of the last German troops and the cautious advance of the first Russian soldiers on a dark, frozen morning. Twenty years later I went to Winston Churchill's funeral. I saw the London house where he died; I walked past his bier in Westminster Hall; I knew that I was a witness to the last great moment of the British Empire. Another twenty-four years later, in 1989, I walked in the streets of the small town where Adolf Hitler was born one hundred years ago. I think I've had enough brushes with history. I do not wish for more." Well, I was wrong.

deed, my own sense of my vocation, differed from those of other émigrés, including those of most refugee historians. They would make their careers and their reputations by teaching and writing and being (or pretending to be) experts in the histories and the politics of the countries they had left behind. This was not what I wanted to do. I did not want to be a historian of Hungary teaching and writing about it to Americans. Perhaps more important: I wanted to be an accomplished English writer. My subjects and my themes would not be Hungarian or Central European or whatnot. (Ah! memories and my appetites: these were, and are, not such simple choices.)

There was, and there still is, only one of my (in 1989 thirteen, and by now more than two dozen) books that I wrote about the history of Hungary. There *was* a kind of patriotic impulse that inspired my writing that book. In the 1970s all kinds of books appeared in the United States and England, celebrating Vienna. Most of their writers were of Viennese origin, once refugees and now historians in America. Their books suggested, indeed, asserted, that around 1900 Vienna was not only an impressive city but the prime jewel of Europe's culture, surpassing even Paris at that fin-de-siècle. (These books then led to the cults of Mahler, Schnitzler, Klimt, et al.). What irritated me that there was almost no mention of Hungary or Budapest in these books—or, if at all, a few patronizing or deprecatory sentences. That was wrong, not only because of the dual structure of the last Habsburg monarchy in which Austria and Hungary were copartners, but because what had happened, especially in Budapest, before and during and after the turn of the century in 1900: a stunning growth of urbanity, learning, civilization, and art to often high levels. That history had to be written. At first, in 1986, I gave that not more than a thought, a one-page proposal for a book, not more. Then the chief editor of a then publisher responded to this offer. That publisher is now defunct but the editor, John Herman, soon became a lifelong friend. I had to go to Budapest for much research and reading. Thither I went for three months in early 1987. The result was *Budapest 1900: A Historical Portrait of a City and Its Culture*, published in New York and London in late 1988.

By that time, 1988, I knew that the Soviet empire and "Communism" (these quotation marks are intentional) were about to break up. Hungarians, congenital pessimists, did not think so. Americans, congenital optimists, did not think so either.* Short-sightedness is of course a physical, an optical condition that can be corrected with glasses. But the eye is not merely a lens or a camera: the functions of seeing and imagining are not successive but simultaneous. Yes, The Wish Is the Father to the Thought: but wishes are complicated things, too, affecting the very act of seeing. Most people think what they prefer to think. Few of them prefer to admit that they see things differently from others.

---

*So declared most Sovietologists; and Robert Gates, head of the Central Intelligence Agency in 1988, secretary of defense of the United States in 2007.

Often they prefer to think that things are worse than they are. Especially Hungarians like to think, and say, that things are hopelessly bad. Is this a low-level sense of Unamuno's wisdom in *The Tragic Sense of Life*? I do not know. What I know is La Rochefoucauld's maxim: "Things are never as good—or as bad—as they seem."

What I know—now—is that the year 1989, my sixty-sixth, was a good one for me. Stephanie and I flew to Ireland and England. I gave a prestigious address in Dublin, lunched amid the roses of Alvilde and Jim Lees-Milne's garden in Badminton across from the palace of the Duke of Bedford, went to Sissinghurst, where Nigel Nicolson walked us through the White Garden and then asked Stephanie to help make lunch (he was much taken by her, less by me), another friend took us to dinner to the Duchess of Kent in Thatched Cottage in Richmond, which was more than pleasant, and then to another dinner at the pompous house of my London (formerly Viennese) publisher in Chelsea, which was not (it was given in honor of a chief editorial writer of the *New York Times* who gave the stupidest and vulgarest toast I have ever heard—I sat at another table and growled, unaware that the New York man's wife was sitting across from me)—all while I was working in the Public Record Office at Kew on *The Duel*, a book which had nothing to do with Hungary. Later that summer a travel magazine sent me to Budapest, whereto I went for a few days in grand hotelian comfort. All of my premonitions were confirmed. Communism had disappeared.

Those few Communists left were no longer Communists. The newspapers were freer and better than ever before (and, alas, after). The coming prime minister and foreign minister, of course non-Communists, I knew well. Lounging in my pajamas early on a radiant morning, looking through the picture window in my de-luxey hotel room, I could see that unique and rather magnificent Budapest sight: the castle hill of Buda, the royal palace being rebuilt, the impressive stone arches of the famous Chain Bridge. Across the bridges and the quays flowed an unending metallic stream of tens of thousands of automobiles, driven and presumably owned by hundreds of thousands of former Communist slaves? No, by Hungarian survivors of what was still called "Communism."

■

I had my friendships, acquaintances, contacts with other Hungarians in the United States and with more in Europe, especially with those who had left Hungary because of its Communization. But there were few Hungarians around where I lived, where my wives and my children were American-born. I did not and do not wish to distance myself from Hungarians—oh, not at all. The few—especially those who were of an older generation, who had known my mother and father—were *so* very dear to me. Many of them lived in Western Europe—Milan, Zurich, Munich—whenever I flew to Europe I flew to them for a warm immersion into more than memories, into a language still filled with remnant but still alive sounds, tastes, touches, including myriad phrases replete with the sensitivities of a society, of a world past. Alas—in the 1980s these men and women began to die away. For those living 1989 was of course a milestone but not a turning point in their lives. One reason for this was that because of the liberalization of the 1970s and 1980s, they had been able to travel to Hungary to see their remaining relatives there, etc., etc., just about every year. Immediately after 1989 they needed not even a visa for Hungary, but that was a very small detail. There had been emigrations of entire classes before—for instance, that of the French aristocracy after the French Revolution, or that of groups of Hungarians after the defeat of their War of Independence in 1849—but then they returned, the French nobles in 1797 and after, the Hungarians in 1867. But in and after 1989 the vast majority of former Hungarians émigrés and refugees chose not to return to living in Hungary. A few of them did; another few devised a compromise, buying or renting an apartment in Budapest whereto they would repair for a few months each year.

What were—what are—the reasons for this general reluctance to return to one's native country? Perhaps nothing much more than the availability of fast air travel? I could not tell. For me, I was never tempted except for one late instance to which I must return (and for which *tempted* is the right word) to return to Hungary: my family and my home are here in Pennsylvania. So in this I differed not from other ex-Hungarians, immigrants, refugees, émigrés. But there had been one substantial difference between my thoughts and those of my former countrymen. They had hoped and looked for every sign, every symptom of a toughening American policy against the Soviet Union; I had looked at and hoped for the contrary. I thought and believed that the destiny of Hungary, within the division of Europe, could and would improve not through a worsening but through an improvement of American-Russian relations. I knew—well before, during, and after the 1956 revolution in Hungary—that the United States would not (and indeed should not) risk a nuclear war against Russia for the sake of Hungary (just as I knew in 1962 that the Russians would never risk a nuclear war with the United States for the sake of Cuba). These were not the sentiments of a pacifist, or of a cautious moderate, which I am not. What I knew was that a lessening of hostilities and restrictions between "West" and "East" in Europe would necessarily lead to a rusting away of the Iron Curtain, and therefore to a weakening of the Russian or Communist grip on Hungary, and on much of Eastern Europe. Under the surface, whatever surface, "Communism" and the Russian empire had begun to crumble. One should encourage their weakness, not freeze them into rigidity.

Among Hungarians, I was rather alone with such views. Fortunately I was not asked for my opinions, so that discrepancy mattered hardly or not at all. But there was one exception of sorts. This was my connection with, indeed, my elective affinity for, an old priest, Father and then Monsignor Béla Varga. I had known him since 1943. He was an important personage in the

Small Holders, a rural agrarian party, democratic and opposed to the Germans, extending itself to an urban and civic section which I "joined" at the age of nineteen. Béla, a son of a peasant family, tall, impressive, blue-eyed, brimming over with the milk of human kindness (which is why I dedicated *Budapest 1900* to him), became the chairman of the elected parliament of Hungary in 1945, fleeing the country two years later and then becoming in New York the head of a Hungarian National Committee, chosen because of his personality and prestige. I saw him here and there during at least three decades; he visited us in Pennsylvania two or three times; we respected, more, loved each other. During the twenty years before the great events of 1989 I saw him more than often. By that time the Hungarian National Committee had ceased to exist, by and large; Béla lived modestly, in two tiny rooms in a convent on 72nd Street run by Hungarian nuns. Whenever I came to New York. I rushed to him on my evenings, to his self-bought Hungarian suppers, in the company of two other émigré Hungarians. One was Imre Kovács, a former leader of the Peasant Party, an extraordinary man and writer, another close friend of mine who died, with tragic suddenness, nine years before he could have returned to Hungary, perhaps in triumph. Another man, Béla's third regular and confidential guest, turned out to be a disappointment, about whom anon. In 1989 it became obvious that the new democratically elected prime minister of Hungary would be József Antall, the son of an upright and honest high civil servant who during the Second World War worked closely with Béla for the purpose of helping and harboring Polish and French and Jewish refugees in Hungary. On the occasion of one of my visits to Hungary in the early 1980s, Béla sent a message to József Antall through me. In April 1990 Antall called Béla to come to Budapest, to preside over the opening of the first democratically elected parliament. Béla asked me to write his opening speech, which I of course did. One April afternoon the telephone rang. He asked that I come with him. My daughter's graduation from college, her wedding, the reception at our house and in our garden were around the corner, due in a few weeks. For a moment I hesitated, but my wife, Stephanie, said: "If he asks you to go you must."

So I went. It was, of course, a starry occasion. The entire government awaited us at the airport. As the old priest, my much loved friend, moved slowly down the steps of the airplane ramp, ·
my eyes were filled with tears, and I thought: what all must course in his head now stepping down onto the soil of his country, thirty-three years after he had been forced to leave it? All went well. It was a sun-laden, very bright morning. We were put in a row of government automobiles, we were put up in a government guest house, high up in the Buda mountains. This was not my first visit to Budapest after my self-chosen exile forty-four years before, but throughout the drive I was flooded by the sense of how the sight and my memories of streets and houses of Budapest affected me: here they were (still?) and here I was (again?). One thing that stunned me were the reactions of my

then friend, the third of our frequent supper companions in Béla's convent rooms. Unlike mine, this was his first return to Hungary. Unlike me, he was thoroughly Hungarian-minded, thinking in Hungarian, a lawyer for Hungarian immigrants in New York through forty years. Yet during the long ride from the airport to the hills I saw (and heard) not the slightest sign (or sound) of emotions on his otherwise far from stoic countenance. Soon there was accumulating evidence that he was moved not by memories of his past but by ambitions for his present and future. These included the profits of his association with Béla. Two days later he elbowed me (and others) aside: he would and did ride to the Parliament in the leading government automobile, at Béla's right side. Presently he became a leader of the Christian-Democratic Party and a member of the new Parliament. Why am I writing this? Because of my recognition of what a complex matter nationalism, in the minds and hands and mouths of politicians, so often is . . .

Anyhow: those were memorable days. Two days after our arrival, the first freely elected Parliament opened. I was made to sit in a royal box, with the daughter of Otto von Habsburg, who knew of me and my Budapest book. I saw Béla clamber up, with some difficulty, to the rostrum that the superintendent of the House helped to build in order to help Béla, who had Parkinson's disease, mount the podium. I heard his speech, including my own words and phrases, lasting for about nine minutes. I was not proud; but I was moved. There followed a reception with champagne, Béla was tired; he asked to be driven back to the guest house to rest. I walked out of the huge Parliament building with my friend Lala (Mándy), an old family friend whom I had discovered living in Munich four years before, a remnant representative, more, a prototype of an old Hungary now gone forever, handsome still, full of the old Hungarian mix of pessimism and panache. I had been able to arrange for him to be with the official escort group, with a seat in yet another royal box. Now we were walking down a quay above the Danube, and we sat down on the terrace of a hotel on a sunny noon hour. Before us the brilliant sparkling scene of the river, the bridges, the palaces, greenery, hills. If only my mother had lived to see this! If only she could see us now! I thought and said (and not for the last time, either). And the night before I dined with Lala and Ila, friends of my mother's, living members of her generation, still kicking. Oh, the past was gone, but not entirely so: no, not at all. There may be expectations of happiness: but happiness itself has only something to do with expectations. Happiness is the sensation of a present moment, at most, of moments. But it is never, never separable from the sense of the past. It has nothing to do with the future: because the past is the only thing that we know.

■

What I did not know—or expect—in 1990 then came about. From then on I would arrive in Hungary every year, in some years even twice. That was, and remains, consequent to something wholly unexpected then. *Each year,* for seventeen years now, beginning in 1991, a book that I had written in English and published in the United States and England, would be translated and published in Budapest. They would be produced in time for the traditional Book Week in early June, when on a principal square in downtown Budapest large crowds mill around and amid a whole forest of white kiosks and tents, where hundreds of authors of a hundred publishers sit for an hour or two, signing and dedicating their books. Now I was (and still am) among them, in virtue of my books with their subjects which had and have very little to do with Hungary. How and why did—why does—this happen? To this day I do not really know. "Because of the way you write"—my friends in Hungary are wont to say. "Because he is a writer rather than a historian"—my nonfriends are wont to say. The voices of the latter I hear seldom, but their echoes, well, sometimes.

Anyhow—so I arrive, each year, sometimes alone, lately with my new wife,* often on a blazing hot June morning, descending on Hungary. Ten or fourteen days later I return home, to Pennsylvania. I choose these words very carefully. I "arrive" in

*D. 5 June 2006. "It was worth to come [to Hungary] for this very day, because we went to the Farkasréti Cemetery with P. on the No. 59 streetcar. And I could not find my father's grave, and then this darling P. found it, the plaque covering the urn. I knelt down and cried bitterly. How I love this good woman: it is such a symptom that *she* found it. She also found a little dry flower wreath that we hung on the stone."

Hungary, where I am now something of a successful author, an "arriviste"—an "arriviste" in spite of myself, in spite of my temperament, in spite of my aspirations: but I cannot escape the thought that whatever my reception may be in Hungary that is due to my reputation from elsewhere, to my having arrived from abroad. And then my "return" is from my native city and country to my home, which is in Pennsylvania. Besides—or not so "besides"—it was during one of those fly / arrive / immerse / return dips into Hungary and Hungarianness that the formula sprang into my mind: Hungary is my mother, America is my wife.

Enough of these ruminations. "Ruminations": do I have, like a cow, two stomachs, a Hungarian and an American one? (Yes, so far as appetites go: there are American dishes that I desire and like as well as I do Hungarian ones.) Instead: let me now try to separate the good from the bad, something that a churning stomach cannot do but a churning heart and mind, perhaps.

I am blessed by the serendipity of Providence, by a reputation there that I am not sure that I deserve while I gulp it down, not at all eagerly but thoughtlessly and quickly. The least important of its results are the Medal of Merit awarded me by the president and government of Hungary in 1994, and the so-called Corvinus Chain, gilt like that of a sommelier but without his cup, in 2001. The most important of my gifts have been my finding and acquiring new friends. In the last seventeen years the few old ones, one by one, disappeared and died. The new ones are much younger than I am. First and foremost among them András Bán, who, at first, was my research assistant when in 1987 I read and read for my *Budapest 1900* at the great Széchenyi Library in the former royal palace, where he also worked: his putting at least a dozen or more books or other volumes on my desk as I arrived each morning was invaluable, and very soon I found that there was much more than that. He was a historian: but his interest in literature and in its inevitable relevances to and evidences for history were similar to mine. Soon I found him to be a close friend. Tall, skeletal, with a deeply lined face, preternaturally wise eyes behind enormous glasses, entirely unassuming, modest, unpretentious, an offspring of provincial parents but with how much refinement in his heart! I helped him and guided him in his work; so did he help mine. I inspired and directed him to books that he wrote. He lived with his older sister, another tall and gangly creature, whose affection for me flowed and flowed because of what she saw as my love and concern for her brother. Around the age of forty she became afflicted with multiple sclerosis; she is still alive; she can hardly move now; she returned to live with their very old and often helpless parents, worshiping at the memory and shrine of her brother. How sad all this is! András was not to live long. Being very Hungarian, he was of course a pessimist throughout his life—the dark clouds in his brain shot through, however, with sudden rays of a skeptical and very fine sense of humor: but no matter now. He was thirty-eight years old, in early 2000, when his stomach troubles were diagnosed as deep-seated cancer of his liver. A few months later he had to give up working altogether. I tried to help him in many ways—no need to describe those attempts here. Now his ailing sister and his mother were living with him in their crowded flat, in a large tenement house, on the edges of Budapest. I came to see them as often as I could. Slowly, gradually, András failed to speak. He died in September 2001, a month after I had left Hungary that year, a month after I saw him last; I remember myself, stumbling disconsolately across the dusty, rundown park stretching from their house to the Metro station. I could not be at his funeral.* His mother and father had a large handsome gravestone made for him in the cemetery of the western Hungarian provincial city where they now live, with the motionless and almost speechless spinster sister. What sadness! What Hungarian sadness! He had become something like my adopted son. (His birthday and my son Paul's birthday are the same, the second of March.) Here at home on my desk stand pictures of my mother, of my wives, and of my children, save for one late sad photo of someone not of my blood family: András. His mother had taken it: he sits, bent on a park bench, alone, pensive, and infinitely sad. I shall never forget him.

And then there have come other friends into my life; my quiet, thoughtful and superb editor and translator, another András

*D. 28 September 2001. "I dreamed that I was with András. We had a nice conversation. I told him that whether he believes in God or not, how can he not believe in the immortality of the human soul? It is palpable. That love survives death is only part and parcel of that."

(Barkóczi); my other editor Miklós (Nagy); and perhaps at least half a dozen others, invaluable because of their intelligence and of their affection for me.* And there is my amazement at the intelligence of many young Hungarians whom I on occasion encounter. In 1991 I taught at two universities: this was the only time since 1990 that I spent in Budapest more than two weeks. Like most students everywhere in the world, there were a few serious students doing their homework while most did not much; but there was one important difference between them and American students. Their writing and spelling were good. I had to correct the contents of their papers but not their language. The high level of secondary-school training still prevailed in Hungary even under Communist regimes; it is weakening now but much of it exists still. I feel fortunate—almost blessed—when I talk (and, yes, listen) to groups of young students there.

And Budapest: its atmosphere and its aspirations, its sounds and smells were and are so different from those of my youth; buildings are rotting but others are being rebuilt and new ones arise, and so many things I saw and liked and disliked in so many ways other than when I was young. Now I was more interested in what was old than in what was new. I had become conscious of a

---

*D. 2 November 2006. (They came to visit me here.) "I am awaiting my two Hungarian friends to arrive this afternoon (all my *old* friends and ties to Hungary gone now). But they, esp. András, are still a v. important and satisfying tie. But the old Hungary, with its associations, gone. Do I have a nostalgia for it? Yes. No."

few places and of their significances I had not thought of before: of their significances because of their history: of dark courtyards, of crumbling backstreets, of houses I had not noticed before. Also: the circumstances of my residences in Hungary have been fortunate. I had enough money. (At least until recently: with the falling worth of the dollar "poor" Hungary now costs me as much as, if not more than, the "rich" United States.) For the past eight years I have stayed in Budapest in a palatial mansion that had once been the house of a once prominent family I knew, built more than eighty years ago. Some of my American family call it a "palace" without much exaggeration: to describe it further, or to describe through what odd coincidence I got there, would be amusing but for these pages too long. Great privacy, comfort, an affectionate staff—but, as the years go on, a growing emptiness . . .* Yes, once in awhile I dine with my wife at Gundel's, where a table at a corner is always reserved for me, the same table where my parents once sat. Yes, on one occasion I gave an Open University lecture (for which, I must say, I prepared assiduously), with an audience of nearly one thousand pressing into a great hall, and then my address was telecast to three million Hungarians. All of this was good and is etched into my memories. One of my blessings: I remember good things better than

*D. 4 July 2001. "Now, when in Budapest, I stay in the empty palatial villa of the Chorins. It is empty, empty of meaning, and I fill it for a few days, from time to time, as a ghost. My presence there would seem to my mother and father so odd, so strange."

bad ones. So let me be impressionist and close this subchapter with five memorable high moments of heartbeat.

There was a summer morning in 1985, still one of those years when I came to Budapest near-anonymous, as a kind of tourist: my wife, my son, my daughter-in-law, and three American friends had come with me for something like ten days. We stayed in a spa-like hotel on Margaret Island. S. had a cough. I took her to the hotel doctor, a woman. We did not have long to wait. I had to translate. There was little conversation. She said that she was also a doctor at a state social insurance corporation, in their building on Fiúmei út. I broke into tears. "That . . . that," I stuttered, "was where my father was a chief physician forty, fifty years ago." Was it only memory that made me tremble and weep? More, I think: it was the serious mien of this spare Hungarian woman doctor. So was my father, serious—two of them, generations apart, incarnations of an old, serious, respectable Hungarian profession. As I left her office, I thought what she must have thought and must still think of me. She was responseless but not indifferent. My wife gave me a Kleenex and told me to blow my nose.

There was that late spring afternoon in 1991. I was living in Budapest for a few months, for the duration of a teaching semester. S. had come to keep me company for two months or so. We arranged to meet at a café in the Inner City at half-past six, she coming by taxi or the subway, I walking through the street from the university building. In 1943, forty-eight years before, it sometimes happened that coming from the university (another building then), I would scurry through that then smartest of shopping streets, Váci-utca, to meet my mother, who, after a session at her hairdresser, sat with friends at Gerbeaud or Floris in Vörösmarty Square, where we would then board the No. 15 autobus and wend home for a late lunch. And now I was hurrying down the same street, from the university—passing, among other things, the hairdresser shop at the same place, with the same name ("Femina") nearly half a century later—to meet S., my winsome American wife with her inimitable smile and demure chic. Of course the street was not the same, Budapest was not the same, Hungary was not the same, the café and the people there were not the same, but I had prepared for this rendezvous with my spirit risen high. We had a drink, and then walked away somewhere for dinner. But that *was* (and still is) one divine high memory of my life. "One's life is a pilgrimage, not a work of art," I wrote later in a sort of diary, "(which is why some of the most intelligent aesthetes and hedonists so often mess up their lives). Still, once in awhile God allows (and inspires) one to add a small bit of *pentimento* to one's life: an overlay, rather than a reconstruction of something that may be sad but that is also beautiful."

There were a few, now memorable half-hours on one or two June afternoons in 1992, 1993, 1994. I write "now," because those half-hours connected two people who are now dead. The half-hours were my walking down on a hill from one of them to the other. Béla, the old priest, had returned to Hungary in 1991.

I had something to do with the complications and the intrigues about where he would then dwell. Eventually the then prime minister arranged for him to live in a villa up on Rose Hill, a government house with plenty of staff who (of course) adored him: but his Parkinson's was well advanced. He could move only with great difficulty, though his mind was good still. He had very few visitors—he was comfortable but a bit forlorn—whenever I arrived in Budapest I sped to him. We had not much left to talk about; at times we sat in silence for long seconds; I held his hands; he kissed me as I said good-bye, then the maid and the janitor walked me out, assuring me that he was really quite well. (He died in 1995: I was able to come to his funeral, which was a grand and lengthy occasion, including numberless bishops and endless speeches. ["Temetni tudunk." "To bury: *that* we Hungarians know how to do"—a national proverb].) They closed the gate behind me. I had a half-hour walk down the winding streets and alleys of the hill, to the large modern building at the bottom on the top of which, in a kind of penthouse, lived Ila. I had hurried up the hill, eager to see Béla; now I was hurrying down the hill, eager to see Ila, both occasions brimful with expectations, though different ones. Ila was not my blood relative but, well, almost. I no longer had any relatives in Hungary. But she was a close friend of my mother's and an even closer friend of Vera, who was the once closest friend of both of them—close enough for Ila to accept the marriage offer by Vera's husband when he became a widower. Of course he was wealthy, and an Italian citizen. I write "of course" because Ila knew her own interests very well. She was sophisticated, intelligent, elegant, demanding, very, very careful with her possessions and money, though not with those of others; acid with her criticism of many people, save for her daughter and granddaughter, two small crystalline vessels wherein she poured just about every drop of her stream of coagulated love. She lived in that once admired modern but now rundown building of the 1930s in considerable comfort, her apartment filled with good furniture and paintings and lacy things, something that she was able to guard and protect and keep even during much of the Communist regime. Now, in 1992, she was again a widow. It was not loyalty, and not even only the memory of my mother, that drove me to her each time, again and again. It was her representation—more, her incarnation—of a world that I had still known: but, more important for me: her language full of acute memories of people, this one or that, previous jewels of souvenirs of men and women, their looks, houses, places—added to those her sharp judgments of men and women still living (including my wife, of whom she was oddly jealous, or perhaps not so oddly: she was now a very old woman, but a woman nonetheless). Before 1994, she would still consent to be taken on occasion to an expensive restaurant or two, ferried there and back by a special taxi she could order by telephone. After that she would no longer leave her cove, waited on by successive nurses around the clock. She died in 2006, my very last living connection with a world, my mother's world—(on 27 September, the same day András had died six years before).

Two more vignettes, both occurring during an episode of my life, the rising and receding tide of my passion for a Hungarian woman. The thirty-first of January 2004 was my eightieth birthday. The night before I was put down on Budapest airport in pitch dark, after a twice-delayed dreadful air journey. Now I awoke on a low bed in her rundown flat. There was a telegram from the president of Hungary, a felicitation for my birthday. The American ambassador invited me (well, now us) for dinner next night. A weak winter sunlight seeped through the gray windows of her main room. It was arrested before the windowless hall that lay dark even at midday. There the radio was on, Hungarian Radio One, its noon program. And—how could I have expected that?—actors and actresses were carefully reading into a microphone portions of the Hungarian translation of my *Confessions* ... And in a minute or two, suddenly my words in Hungarian, beautifully intoned, the entire page I had written about my Jewish grandparents, of who they were, fifty or more years ago including this sentence: "They were the most admirable people I have ever known." And now one, perhaps two, perhaps three million Hungarian people could hear these words! *They* could not. I broke down and cried.

Later, during a bitter month I spent in Budapest, I had to sign my books in a bookshop. The end of a weary weekday that was, ugly skies, low clouds, splashing rain. A routine task for me that was, one during each of my visits to Hungary; and now after I had coursed across the city for hours. But people came, one after another, coming from work: simple people, men and women, old and young, students, not academics, buying and paying for my books, and then uneasily standing in a line, all of them modest, some of them slightly embarrassed, so grateful for my rapid scrawl on the title pages of my books they had just bought. My heart rose in a large tide of gratitude to them. They thought that they owed me something: but they did not. I owed something to *them*. An hour so passed. The rain had stopped. Ashes and cinders; I stepped out and then forth on that murkiest of pavements on that grayest of boulevards in that grayest of cities toward a garish shrieking square and then a streetcar stop.

■

The past is the only thing we know. The past is the only thing anyone knows. It is only that some of us are more conscious of that than are others. Thence the attractions of some remnants of the past for us: the sight of certain old houses, the courtesies of certain waiters, the taste of certain old dishes, our native language, a few gravestones. Enough to pull hundreds of thousands of men and women once born in Hungary from across the Alps, the Channel, over entire oceans, the Southern Hemisphere, each year. Not enough to make them stay for good.

The reasons for that are complicated, they vary. In my case, the temptations to move back to Hungary—that, too, only temporarily, perhaps for a few months each year?—existed, here and there, but they were weak. The pull of my family, my house, my place in Pennsylvania—and of the English language—has been strong. But there were and there are other reasons too.

Hungary is now becoming—faster and faster—a new, a classless society. There are a few rich, there are still many poor. I know almost no one of the new rich, and no one of the truly poor. But soon these extremes of a social scale will disappear. There will always be a few (honest?) rich but—perhaps—fewer and fewer honest poor. I guess this is a good thing: as Tocqueville thought, perhaps even so ordained by God. It will be a Hungary even more different than it is now, even more different than it was during the worst years of Communism, ever more different for me. As a matter of fact, I shall not live to see it.

There will always be some kind of ruling class, rulers and ruled (the future composition of that does worry me). But before that there is one condition, a historical circumstance about which I am more optimistic than are Hungarians, and also more optimistic of the destiny of my native than of that of my adopted country. The United States is now way beyond the Bourgeois Era, its society, its structure, its politics, its manners and morals. The United States had a, by and large, bourgeois period, an interlude, perhaps, from about 1870 to 1950, from the end of the Civil War to the end of the Second World War, but that is now over. For the United States the entire Modern or Bourgeois Age, that of the past five hundred years, is over. What has been happening in the United States for at least two generations now is an ever increasing, indeed, overwhelming evidence of something that, again, Tocqueville saw: that the character of a people is more important than are their institutions.

Hungary, four thousand miles away, between Central and Eastern Europe, has not yet entered the Bourgeois Age. And will it—ever? Its bourgeois, or middle (the two terms are not the same but let that now go), classes are weak. They were further reduced, maimed, decimated, during Hungary's ever so tragic twentieth century. And now the proletariat has begun to dwindle. Many of the poorest have become middle class—well, in a way. They are now accustomed to supermarkets, television, airports, computers, vacations, more and more of them have their own cars. That is all to the good—well, at least probably so. There are still many things in which Hungary has to catch up with "the West." But its people show more and more signs of classlessness, less and less of anything that was once bourgeois (both in the bad and in the good sense of that word). One evidence: the clothes people now wear. But then, the cult of sloppiness, ugliness, even brutality is there in Paris or New York, too.*

More important than the measure of their material goods is

---

*D. 7 June 2007: "I saw not *one* elegant woman in Budapest. Hordes of women and girls in those awful toreador pants. . . . Men and boys half-naked, hairy legs, dirty feet, often unshaven: girls dressed up (up?) clinging to them. But that is now a near-universal phenomenon."

what people think and believe—a condition that may be even more important in Hungary than it is in other countries. Which brings me to politics—or, rather, to the rhetoric of politics. The now increasingly popular political party calls itself conservative, civic (*polgári*), bourgeois. Its loudest spokesmen are not that. They are nationalist, and populist. This is not the place to describe, or even to sum up the history of Hungarian politics and elections during the past twenty years. But it may be the place to sum up my disappointments. Very soon, perhaps even at the very time of the regime change in 1989, I thought that all of those, mostly liberal, Experts and Political Scientists and Economists and Futurologists (vide Francis Fukuyama and his idiotic *The End of History*, 1990) were wrong. (Twenty years later they are the selfsame recognized Experts. Of course.) Their cheers rang to the rafters: Liberalism and Parliamentary Democracy have arrived in Eastern Europe, a tide sweeping the Soviet Union too, perhaps the entire world. Yes: there were now new political parties, parliaments, elections, universal suffrage, freedom (?) of the press, etc.: renewed or new institutions, some of them even with respectable traditions. But what of the characters who were crowding into them? Their ambitions were not only inseparable from, they were stoked with their suspicions and hatreds for their political and ideological opponents. Very soon men who had been the closest friends, sincere associates and brave allies during their struggles under or against the one-party regime before 1989 now stopped, indeed, refused, to speak to former friends whom they saw as—or even suspected of—belonging to another party; attributing to them the lowest of possible motives and the worst of possible corruptions. Party leaders in Parliament ordered their deputies to turn their backs to their former friends of other parties, to refuse to shake hands with them. "We" and "They" is not only the rule: it is the essence of political and, alas, intellectual life in Hungary now. "They" are not only the parliamentary or party opposition; "they" are not opponents but traitors; "they" are not "real" Hungarians. Some of this "we" and "they" filtered through and down, too, to the swampy ground of anti-Semitism (or, perhaps more precisely: Judaeophobia)— something especially lamentable in Hungary, where people of Jewish origin still amount to about one per cent of the population. This has gone and goes together with the inclination of the so-called "conservatives" not only to blame everything on Communists and Liberals, but with a large and vague tendency to idealize, at least indirectly, much that had existed in "Christian" and "national" Hungary before 1945, before the Russian occupation and the subsequent imposition of Communist rule.*

Such are the political and ideological and intellectual hatreds in Hungary now. In October 2006, on the fiftieth anniversary of

*That was, and remains, falsifying history: since in Hungary many awful things had occurred during and toward the end of the Second World War, including the deportation and then the mass murder of about half of Hungarian Jews: a chapter in the history of a people who—unlike most Germans—have not yet swallowed, let alone digested, the memory and the meaning of that.

the great national Rising of 1956 (when, for once, the great majority of the nation had been united), angry crowds were roaming and ravaging through streets in Budapest. Nearly two decades after the "liberation" of Hungary from the remnants of Communism, discussion, let alone compromise or reconciliation between the two camps, is now, more than ever before, impossible.* At the same time it seems that, at least until now, the mass of this now increasingly classless (though by no means homogeneous) Hungarian people are uninterested (at best), or numbed (at worst) by this agitated rumble of ideological rhetoric—alas, most (though not all) of it coming from the "conservative" Right. How long this condition will last, I cannot know. What I know is that this tendency for disastrous politics, for desperate suspicions, for deadening accusations, compromising the health and mutilating the reputation of an entire nation, has been endemic in the political history of Hungary in the past. But, then, history remains unpredictable; and, while some of its conditions do, history does not really repeat itself—except in the minds of those who do not know it or who do not wish to know it well enough or at all. Perhaps new Hungarian generations will rise, struggling against their unjust limitations and frustrations, but not altogether suffused with a fatal pessimism, fatal suspicions, fatal hatreds. There are some signs of that. Or: so I hope.

---

*D. 21 February 2004. "Important observation: it is easier to be sincere in America than it is here [in Hungary]."

Hatred and fear. It was about ten years ago—and then not because of Hungary—that a, I think important, discovery, rather
than an invention: a recognition, rather than an intellectual construct, crystallized in my mind. This was that though "Right"
and "Left" have become more and more inaccurate, imprecise,
and even senseless categories, still it may be detected that Fear
dominates the "Left" and Hatred the "Right" among many peoples of the world. I have written about this. I also know that this
is a very broad and sweeping generalization. Also, that these fundamental inclinations are not whole, because there is fear within
hatred and there is hatred within fear—for such is the complex
alchemy of the human mind. Still: which of the two dominates?
Chesterton wrote once that it is hatred that unites people, while
love is always individual. (I would write: personal.) Going beyond Chesterton, I think—and, yes, I fear—that Hatred is ever
stronger, and therefore ever more attractive than Fear—which
is, among other things, why women may admire a man who hates
but not one who fears, which is how Hitler was the greatest revolutionary in an entire century, which is how and why the so-
called extreme Right in Hungary now attracts youth while the
extreme Left is largely extinct; which is, too, why a pervasive ideology of extreme anti-Communism caused much harm in the
United States, uniting hundreds of millions of Americans, as it
brings together many Hungarians now, including young people
who have not experienced or known Communism in their lives.

Nationalism, instead o f patriotism: the first is populist and modern, the second was traditionalist and old; the former a cult of "the people," the latter the love of a country. Hence my anxieties in Hungary and in America: in my native country and in my adopted one. And there remains a melancholy sum total of a question: Is Hungary closer to me now than it was before 1989? Yes.* Will I—can I—return there? No longer—no.

*D. 14 June 2006. "I read about the dreadful, nigh unbelieveable, tragedy of a good and decent family in Transylvania [the Óvárys], one or two nights after the Russians arrived. How much I feel for them, how I wish to belong w. them, which of course is utterly impossible, as it was before too. The strange self-carved path of my life. Less than an honest pilgrimage. (An escape, rather.)"

FIVE

Intermezzo:
My Churchill Saga

I was sixteen years old in Hungary in 1940, when Hitler's Germans conquered Europe and marched into Paris. Few Americans know what it meant to live in the middle of Europe then; few of them know it now. Our forlorn hopes focused on Churchill. My mother adored him. I was a budding historian then, silly about many things, and with vast gaps in my knowledge of the world; but one thing I understood even then is how close Hitler came to winning the Second World War. What I did not know then was that Roosevelt and Stalin would win the Second World War. What I knew then and what I know now is that Churchill was the one who did not lose it.

Five years later the war was over. I had not lost my life, but I lost my native country; I chose to flee from it to America and to become a professional historian. Ever since then, my memories and my knowledge of May and June 1940 have been burning in my mind, in a symbiotic way: my memories have not faded as my knowledge about history has increased—but are memory and knowledge different? Yes and no.

From dribs and drabs of all kinds of reading, I began to suspect that, before Churchill rose to become a heroic figure in 1940, his position was by no means as strong and secure as it appeared a few months later. But that suspicion was part and parcel of a larger and more definite knowledge, which was that Hitler could have very well won the Second World War in 1940 (and even 1941); and that, therefore, there was this Last European War, 1939–41, before Pearl Harbor, a detailed and structured history of which ought to be written.

That took me almost six years, interrupted by the illness and death of my first wife in 1970. Then I had a stroke of luck. That year the British government decided to shorten the closure of government documents from fifty to thirty years. Thereby the papers from 1940 were available for researchers in 1971. I spent three weeks of a hot summer in London in the old Public Record Office and found what I wanted—most of the War Cabinet records of late May 1940. Yes—Churchill's situation before and during the first days and nights of Dunkirk was insecure, to say the least. Most of the Conservatives in Parliament accepted his prime ministership reluctantly; his appointment was followed by disaster after disaster on the fronts; his determination to keep fighting, at no matter what cost, seemed less and less reasonable or promising. But while he was determined, Hitler was hesitant, not quite sure what to do before Dunkirk. Still, I could not devote more than three pages to that dramatic contrast; I was, after all, writing a book about an entire continent and about more than two years of a world war: *The Last European War: September 1939–December 1941*.

Twelve years later, I returned to Churchill. My then editor at Ticknor and Fields, John Herman, agreed to my proposal to write *The Duel: The Eighty-Day Struggle Between Churchill and Hitler*. Again I spent a fair amount of time in the Public Record Office, now in Kew, found even more documentary evidence than before, and wrote some fifteen pages about those crucial days of May 1940. I had an advantage that I had not had in 1971, which was photocopying. But when I finished the final draft of *The Duel*, I threw the accumulated mess of those photocopied pages away. That was a foolish thing to do, because eight years later I chose to write yet another book, concentrating on a day-by-day (and sometimes hour-by-hour) reconstruction of what happened in London from 24 May to 28 May in 1940.

During those secret War Cabinet sessions there occurred a verbal duel, not between Churchill and Hitler but between Churchill and Lord Halifax, the foreign secretary who—and let me say, not quite unreasonably—was convinced that Churchill was hotheaded; that, in that given and dangerous situation, there ought to be at least a crack open in the British door, to ascertain what Hitler would want from Britain. But Churchill, warm-

hearted rather than hotheaded, was right. He pulled through—
by a hairbreadth, not more.

Those five days were dramatic. No one knew about that drama
beyond the War Cabinet: not Roosevelt, not the Americans, no
one among the press lords and journalists in Britain. It is curious
why Churchill wrote nothing about this in his, now immortal,
second volume of *The Second World War.* I think that there were
two reasons—purposes—for his relative silence. One was educa-
tional. He knew that he wished to bequeath to the English-
speaking peoples of the world an impression that the entire
people of Britain were splendidly united during those perilous
days. Yet some—and perhaps more than a few—weren't. His
other purpose—or, rather, in this case, his motive—was, or must
have been, his magnanimity. He chose to write nothing about his
then so decisive and profound disagreement with Halifax. (He
once said to his daughter, who repeated this to me: "Never say to
anyone, 'I told you so.'") He wrote in the preface of *The Second
World War:* "I do not describe it as history, for that belongs to another generation. But I claim with confidence that it is a contribution to history which will be of service for the future." This,
for once, was too modest. My contribution was to describe those
crucial days in some detail. And—to insist on their meaning: to remind people—and perhaps especially English people—how very
close that was, how close was Hitler then to winning that war.

Five Days in London: May 1940 was a modest success. Two days
after September 11, 2001, Giuliani, the mayor of New York, held

it up before the television cameras, declaring how inspired he was reading about Churchill and British courage during the London Blitz in 1940. Well, there is not one word about the Blitz in *Five Days* . . . but no matter: The next day multiple book orders began to flicker on the screens of the Yale University Press offices in New Haven. "Will your next book be *Three Hours in London*?" a friend asked. "No, it won't," I said.*

Now something else was happening. During the ten years between *The Duel* and *Five Days*, I worked on a study of Hitler and his biographers. Among other things, my reading and research confirmed another related matter, which I had known but to which I had not devoted too much attention before: that Hitler hated Churchill more than he hated others among his great adversaries† (he had a considerable respect and even liking for Stalin); that many Germans, and not only neo-Nazis, had similar inclinations; that sympathizers of Hitler and of the Third Reich, such as David Irving, thought it best to whiten Hitler's reputation by blackening Churchill's. And then, Marlis G. Steinert, a fine scholar and one of the better Hitler biographers, directed me to something peculiar and disturbing. The papers of the high Gestapo chief, Heinrich Müller (who may have been brought se-

---

*Well—I later did—not without some reluctance—write a small book, *Blood Toil, Tears, and Sweat*, dealing with the circumstances and the meaning of Churchill's first speech after he had become Prime Minister, on 13 May 1940.

†Goebbels after talking with Hitler on 18 June 1941, about Churchill: "Were it not for him, this war would have ended long ago."

cretly to the United States after the war by Allen Dulles), were published by a small right-wing publisher in California. They included the transcripts of two secret telephone conversations between Churchill and Roosevelt.

I had known about those. Technicians of the German Ministry of Posts had established a listening station on the North Sea coast of Holland, where they were occasionally able to break into secret telephone lines in London. One transcript of a Churchill-Roosevelt conversation (on 28 July 1943) had been printed in a German collection of documents; it seemed authentic. But this was different. In these Müller "transcripts," Churchill appeared brutal, ordering assassinations, conspiring with Roosevelt about what might happen at Pearl Harbor, etc. I found his very language implausible. I tried to look into the matter, including a search for the original Post Ministry transcripts in various German archives. I found nothing.

Then I struck gold. Through the Lady Soames, née Mary Churchill, Winston's surviving daughter, I got in touch with an Englishwoman who had had the authority to listen in to the secret Churchill-Roosevelt telephone talks as a "censor." She remembered them more than a half-century later. She assured me that the "documents" were false from beginning to end. I wrote a brief article about this skullduggery in *American Heritage* (November–December 2002). Alas, there were, and are still, historians who have used the Müller documents for their own purposes. (The great Spanish historian Altamira once wrote that history consists of more than documents—not to speak of falsified ones.)

I did not bother to recount this matter in a small book of essays, *Churchill: Visionary. Statesman. Historian.* (2002), which included my own diary entries about Churchill's funeral in 1965* (to which I had flown with my eight-year-old son from Toulouse, France, where I had been serving as a Fulbright professor that year). But during my reading for a long chapter, "Churchill's Historianship," something else caught my attention. I had known that, alone among Western statesmen, Churchill showed a fair amount of sympathy and understanding for the situation of my native country, Hungary, even during the Second World War. Reading and rereading the more than two thousand pages of his *Marlborough: His Life and Times*, I was stunned to find that he had written many pages about Hungary in the early eighteenth century, at a time when few, if any, people in Western Europe had any knowledge, let alone interest, in the fortunes and political conditions of that country. Churchill's writing reflected a not in-

*D. 31 July 2004. "Richard Holmes, an English historian, in his *In the Footsteps of Churchill*, 2005, p. 19: 'I cannot hope to improve on the words by the Hungarian-American John Lukacs in his elegiac memoir of a cold, quiet, and solemn day in London, 30 January 1965. "He loved life very much, and he made life possible for many of us because he had a very old, and very strong belief in the possibilities of human decency and of human greatness. . . . In the long and slow and sad music of humanity he once sounded an English and noble note which some of us were blessed to receive and to remember."'"

considerable amount of knowledge, let alone insight and understanding. Subsequently I proposed and then gave a talk at the
British embassy in Budapest about "Churchill and Hungary." It
was then that a thought occurred to me: Why not name a street
after him in Budapest? There would be a proper place for that.
The great Chain Bridge, connecting Buda and Pest, planned and
commissioned by the great Anglophile Hungarian historical personality, Count István Széchenyi, was built by a Scottish engi-
neer, Adam Clark, after whom a square is still named at the Buda
bridgehead. Why not name a "Churchill Square" on the Pest
side of the bridge? I took the liberty of proposing that to the
mayor's office.

Nothing happened for awhile, and I could devote no attention
to it: my darling second wife fell ill and died five months later.
Then another idea: fly to Budapest and make my proposal again
(this time on paper, summing up Churchill's interest and sympa-
thies for Hungary) and then play a trump card. "You do this—
and I shall bring Churchill's daughter to Budapest for the inauguration." They jumped at it. No, a Churchill bridgehead won't
work; but an attractive small street, a Churchill Walk, would be
established in the City Park. "All right," I said. A good friend of
mine approached a famous Hungarian sculptor to make a
Churchill bust, to be erected in a small bower along that Churchill Walk, and in time for Lady Soames's visit and the inauguration on 24 June 2003.

So it happened. There came a social whirl. The Hungarian

ambassador and his wife in London gave a dinner for Mary Soames, with a dozen Englishmen and Englishwomen who knew her and me, and what a sprightly occasion that was! Two days later we were flown to Budapest, gossiping and drinking champagne on the plane. That night there was a box for us in the Budapest Opera, its interior all raspberry-colored marble, to hear Tchaikovsky's *Pique Dame*, which was interminably long and wearisome but no matter.* The day of the inauguration was very hot, and the mayor spoke much too long. Again, no matter. The Hungarian national anthem and "God Save the Queen" were played. I was moved to tears.

Two days later I bid good-bye to Mary.† I told her how grateful I was to her, but also that a chapter of my life had now closed. I am not a Churchill specialist, and I shall write nothing more about her father. But now there is a walk named after him and a

---

*D. 22 June 2003. "Tchaikovsky ought not have written operas and, besides, at times his music is vulgar. Mary did her homework, brought entire English synopsis of plot, (*very*) complicated. Then we are driven to Gundel's, where the two of us sit and dine at now my (once my mother's) table. If only she could see this . . . But is 'see' the right word? I believe that there *is* another world; but whether she sees it or not, perhaps—perhaps—she'll '*know*.'"

†D. 26 June 2003. "Last night, before a small farewell dinner with Alex, another reception forced upon us. I was nervous and fretful. In the car I to Mary: 'I was impatient.' Mary: 'Yes, you were.' I: 'I may have one excuse. People who knew your father sometimes said that he could be very impatient.' Mary puts her hand on my arm: 'But John. He was a *great* man.'"

statue of him in my native city. Things have come full circle. A chapter of my life, in the odd way in which personal and professional intertwine, has ended.

It had not. Two days after I returned to Budapest, both my fax and telephone rang. Young vandals, most presumably devotees of the former Hungarian National Socialist Arrow-Cross Party, had poured red paint over Churchill's bust, tied the ribbon from a wreath around his neck, and scrawled a swastika and a six-pointed Jewish star on the marker of the Churchill Walk. Was this a coda, or an epilogue, to that chapter of my life? Or more than that? By coincidence I had just finished reading Günter Grass's *Crabwalk*, dealing with young neo-Nazis, in which the last sentences are: "It is not over. It will never be." I feel this in my bones and see it clearly.*

"The bitter wind that spoils the sunshine."

I visit the statue almost every year.

*D. 9 July 2003. "So my Churchill saga is not over, it has now this coda—no, more than that . . . And yet: another telephone call from Budapest, as I write, the statue and the marker have been cleaned up in less than a day, a group of citizens helped."

SIX

The World Within Me:
Wives and Loves

■

The purpose of this chapter, as of this book, is not autobiography: it is the history of my thoughts and beliefs, rather than the story of my life. If so—why then a chapter about Wives and Loves? Well ... but aren't loves and wives results of one's thoughts, of which one's physical appetites are consequences, more often than the other way around? And there is another purpose too. I feel compelled to describe—describe rather than define, describe rather than record—what I owed and still owe to my three wives. And so three portraits will follow.

■

Love has its history, like everything else. I do not mean the history of marriages, of courtships, of seductions, of sexual habits, etc., etc. I mean: how men and women saw and loved each other.

That has changed through the ages. For one thing, Romantic Love was a Western European creation, largely extinct now—though not entirely and perhaps not forever. However: love includes, it may even be the result of, class-consciousness, which is what most novels have been about. (It is possible that the lique-faction of classes may have had much to do with the liquefaction of romantic love.) However: love has nationality too. An Italian man and an American woman, or an American man and an Italian woman—but when? 1800? 1920? 1980? Never the same. "Ces sont les nuances qui querrellent, pas les couleurs." Shades of differences matter more than a clash of colors. If God is in the details, so is love.

There is no really first-rate book about the relationships of men and women of different nationalities. Their attractions—attractions of what is unusual, what is slightly exotic, what is extraordinary—are obvious, since curiosity is a vital ingredient of sexual attraction (especially for women), and when that is compounded by vanity (usually for men), God help their beholders: some kind of love will occur, and soon. All of this is infinitely more complex, deeper than sex. Flirtations, courtships, love affairs, marriages between men and women of different nationalities: they may be described amusingly but seldom well enough. Henry James lived in the middle of such matters, but did he really understand them? I think he didn't. Besides: a love affair or a marriage may be punctuated by sudden marvelous mutual understandings, or by (not always sudden, and less marvelous) mis-

understandings: but—and this is a large "but"—not all of the understandings are good, and not all of the misunderstandings are
bad. (Women like men who understand women; but they do not
necessarily like a man who understands *them*.)* When a woman
realizes that her man has misunderstood what she had done or
said or meant, she may be disappointed or angry: but in another
instance she may find that allowable, or perhaps even charming.

Enough of this. One generalization (of which a myriad of exceptions exist, of course): marriages between European men
and American women tend to turn out better than those between American men and European women. But, then, what is
"European"? A Swedish lover is not like a Hungarian one.
(Necessarily? Never?) And what is "American"? All three of
my wives—Helen, Stephanie, and Pamela (H., S., and P.)—
have been American. (H.'s ancestry was more Anglo-Saxon than
Anglo-Norman, with a fair amount of Scots blood too. S.'s ancestry was Anglo-Saxon, with some Pennsylvania-German blood
on her mother's side. P.'s ancestry: Anglo-Saxon and Anglo-
Norman, with perhaps a touch of Indian-Appalachian blood?
Who knows?) Much of this was, and remains, irrelevant. Why
did I not marry Hungarian women? Well, there were just about
none of such around where I lived: but there was more than that
too. Beyond (or beneath?) their various charms there was my

---

*D. 8 March 2001. "We, men, may like a woman who understands us but we
do not particularly like women who understand men."

wives' Americanness that I found attractive. But then Americanness is both less and more than a nationality. What were, what are, its ingredients?

■

History and tragedy—two elements in the destiny of my first wife. History and tragedy: because she incarnated a kind of America that would disappear at the very time she would die: and because she died too young, too soon.

She was dark-haired, serious, with lovely limbs and unusually large brown eyes that her children inherited. She had inherited a certain round-facedness from both of her parents, but then she blossomed to become very beautiful after her wedding, and then both her face and her figure assumed something of a patrician look. (She who had not a drop of German blood was twice mistaken for a Bavarian or Austrian countess.) The birth of both of our children—more than twelve years apart—took an odd toll on her body; she died two years after she bore our daughter, Annemarie. But what a devoted, what a responsible mother she was, and would have remained, into a middle age that she would have borne—another matter I know—with an exceptional kind of serene equanimity. But she was not to live long.

Her parents inherited the advantages and the handicaps of well-to-do provincial American families of a certain period: but very wealthy they were not, nor socially very prominent in Philadelphia. They came from the same background, Pennsylvanians, but utterly unsuited to each other. Helen's mother's parents had died when she was a young child, she was brought up by a grandparent and by relatives, she inherited plenty of money and was sent to good schools and colleges; but she was dreadfully unsure of herself, replete with fears. Helen's father was rubicund: his mind, heart, face, temperament were crimson, awash with red blood: a brilliant student, a brilliant lawyer, a brilliant public official, ready to cut corners and step on his opponents' toes. Among other steps of his career, he, though a Republican, was chosen by Franklin Roosevelt to be Commissioner of Immigration. Among other choices of his life was a Viennese woman who had once been married to a prince; this princess was his mistress during the last fifteen years of his life that, too, was not as long as it should or could have been: he died suddenly, at sixty-two.

From her father Helen inherited the strength of her mind. Her independence of mind, too, though that developed gradually. Her parents' separation occurred when she was very young. She suffered through that, living with her mother, not with her father: the former she respected, the latter she respected and adored. She knew that though they were well off she had, or would have, little in common with her schoolmates, Philadelphia debutante girls primping and ready to "come out." The Springside School in Chestnut Hill gave her a good education; she was at the top or close to the top of her class in 1944, when she was among the but three or four who would go on to college, a small minority of "brains" among the two dozen or more debutantes whose destinies at that time were directed to parties rapidly followed by marriages, not to colleges at all. She went on to Smith, majoring in English, again a very good student, close to the top of her class. (At least one of her professors, a well-known scholar, remembered her many years later.) Then for a couple of years she became a secretary at the Institute for Advanced Studies in Princeton. For a while, T. S. Eliot, a visiting professor there then, chose her for his secretary. At about twenty-five she became a junior editor of the *Ladies Home Journal* in Philadelphia. She kept this job for more than a decade, for a few years even after the birth of our son. It was a routine job, mostly reading unsolicited manuscripts (among which she made at least a few publishable discoveries), but wearisome too, mostly because of the petty envies and intrigues of some of the women editors there. Much of that she recognized: but she kept with them. Her mind was independent but not rebellious. Only those who knew her well—and there were not many—would become aware of qualities of her mind that were inseparable from the, when apparent, stunning qualities of her character.

But then the tragedies of her family accumulated to an extent that she could hardly bear—though bear them she did. She was very different from her siblings, who were also very different from each other. Her oldest brother, a wild and willful young man, inherited his father's temperament but not his brains: one bright spring night, drunk, he fast drove his car into a tree and died in an instant, a month before our wedding. Her second brother, who inherited all of the anxieties and unsureness of his mother, was a severe schizophrenic. Of him his mother was both ashamed and afraid. She had put him away in one mental hospital after another, until his father chose to install him with a helper at the "farm," the country place where the father, prodded and inspired by his princess-mistress, had built a new house. H.'s sister, the youngest of four children, was temperamental and envious (though eventually she bore and brought up five good children). Matters tragic then came to a head in the summer of 1955, two years after our wedding, after the sudden death of H.'s father. His considerable income and wealth vanished, sequestrated by the government. His wife's wealth was unaffected since they were not yet divorced and he had not yet made a will. With a little help from her mother, H. and I could have kept up Anderson Place and her afflicted brother Joe, since Anderson Place belonged legally to him, on account of which the government could take only what was not real estate, only the extensive farm equipment and cattle, etc. But the suspicions of H.'s mother and the jealousies of her sister ruled. They did not want us to have anything to do with Anderson Place, and so its 136 acres and fine buildings were sold. Joe was sent to a state mental hospital. His mental illness had temporarily worsened. Then, after a few years, H. took it upon herself to get him out of the state mental hospital; to get him to a private psychiatrist; to get him to complete his long-before interrupted high-school career by graduating through a correspondence course; to get him an apartment of his own; to help get him a job; to get him to learn to drive a car; to get him to buy a car. He showed her some gratitude: but then such was the effect of the frozen fences of his mind. He would visit us from time to time, sometimes for Christmas too. My second wife, Stephanie, was kind to him. He survived H. by twenty-two years.

Somewhere, perhaps not that deep down, H. had something like a historical sense of what the dissolution of her family meant. Did she have a nostalgia for her childhood when her parents had still been, so to speak, together? I do not think so. What I know is that she evinced no illusions for some idyllic kind of American past lived and experienced by her immediate ancestors. She understood too much about the fatal limitations of their perspectives, of their characters, of human nature, of the United States of America, of the world. This somber kind of knowledge may have helped her to bear the stunning shock of her father's death and what instantly followed it. But another element that sustained her was her then successful pregnancy (she had a miscarriage before) and the imminent birth of our son, nine months after that family earthquake in July 1955. As for all women, motherhood for her was a task for which she prepared and then bore it and carried it on. But for her there was something else too. It gave her an aim, a goal, a full sense of her destiny. The independence of her mind did not pull her in the direction of a career. Her belief of what women were capable of was modern; of what the primary meaning of their life should be, old-fashioned. Her integrity was such that she saw no contradiction between these two, seemingly contradictory, judgments.

Our marriage was not idyllic—not many marriages are—but it was solid, unbroken, because we respected each other in so many ways; and we learned much from each other. She was attracted by my loquacious outspokenness, which, at least in the beginning, she saw as a virtue. In addition to my Europeanness or Hungarianness, she much appreciated how many of our opinions and judgments about things American, about political and intellectual matters, about many kinds of people, agreed. She also tried to accommodate herself and the circumstances of our life to my wants and wishes: for instance, to my desire to keep living in the country despite its difficulties, and on occasion to travel. But—did I know this then? I am certain of it now—I learned more from her than she learned from me. She taught me understatement. She read much of what I wrote and what I tried to write: she was, at times, appalled by the undisciplined method or lack of method in expressing my thoughts on paper. She taught me something that I then learned gradually, and from which later I profited so much—that one must *not* tell readers everything that one knows, even when one knows, or one thinks one knows, interesting connections between disparate things. Yes, there were occasions when she did not understand my stabs of sudden insight or my excited recognitions of such connections. But her corrections went beyond and beneath my writing; they involved my speaking, my behavior. It was not her concern for manners or her sense of proportion when she, from time to time, said that I should not have said or done this or that. She knew something that I came to understand only later: that there is an unsure and anxious selfishness in the need to tell others all that one knows. *She* knew much more than what she would reveal; she amounted to so much more than she perhaps seemed.*

My Hungarianness, driving my mood at times to extremes, from high intoxications of spirits to bitter feelings of dark despair, was something with which she (unlike my two successive wives) could not cope. Was this because she was Protestant, Anglo-Saxon, American, English-speaking and -feeling, so less emotional than her husband? Probably so. But did this constricted range of her feelings mean that the spirit of her Hungarian husband was better than hers? No: because more important than the (horizontal) ranges of mind are the (vertical) depths of

---

*One example. In Paris, in 1965, we were invited to an elegant dinner (unexpectedly, I think, in honor of my Americanness) in a large apartment, great white wings of doors thrown open to make one large room of two. With two tables for twelve guests each, I was seated at our hostess's right at one, she at her host's right at the other: I could see her from a distance. The women at her table, *tout-Paris*, knew English well enough, but kept on *en haut* with their bitchy selfishness, talking nothing but French. But I saw H., who habitually spoke French with some caution and hesitation, holding her own, talking animated French with ease. I was proud of her beyond belief.

character. Her integrity, her honesty, were better, because deeper, than mine.

I had a few social ambitions. She had none. We had little money, we lived in an odd, unfinished house at the edge of a road, much of our land still overgrown with weeds. I was not a snob, or at least I think I was not, but I desired the company of the young, upper-class (when such a designation still made *some* sense) American couples who lived near us then, who led a faster, spendthrift, sometimes even raffish and frivolous partying existence; who accepted, at least on occasions, our presence. H. followed me, at times uneasily, because of her willingness to accommodate herself to my wishes. Within reason: for she would often remind me that we were not like those others, we had so much less money than they had. She was more right than wrong. As the years passed, a few of those people grew closer to us; among other things they began to respect my Europeanness, my authorship, our traveling. But only the very best among them came close enough to her to find and appreciate the qualities of her mind and of her character. Sometimes, at a fancier or richer party where we were among the guests we felt near-outsiders, we were alone. But we were, we remained, together. She who knew my faults and resigned to live with some of them, had perhaps a few shortcomings: but faults? no, none at all.

Soon after our son was born her recurrent illnesses began, usually when autumn or winter set in. The symptoms were recurrent but there was no overall and satisfactory diagnosis. She was told that she could have no more children, but the doctors were wrong. More than twelve years after Paul, our daughter, Annemarie, was born. H.'s care and concern for Paul were truly extraordinary. Among other things there was her home-schooling of him when we were living in France, in addition to his regular enrollment in a French school. Paul was eight years old then. Was she a frustrated woman pouring out her love on a son? I do not think so. The capacity of her heart was larger than that. But there *was* an increasing somberness in her mind, a darkening pessimism underlying her otherwise so impressive characteristic of reserve. It had something to do with her clear view of the world she was now living in. She was profoundly conservative—in the proper and best sense of that word that began to become corrupted in the 1950s. She gave up her outside employment, her editorial job, at the very time (the early 1960s) when millions of American women, wives and mothers who had moved to the suburbs, suddenly felt constrained with what life in the suburbs offered to them, and fled their daytime loneliness to their employment in various offices. H. thought, and often said, that to be ("to be," rather than "to stay") at home with a family was the best employment that a woman could choose. She was a traditionalist. She was a patriot. And a Democrat, and a liberal. She was appalled by the Vietnam War, and by Nixon and Kissinger. She disdained American nationalism and sentimentalism. "The American Dream" was a phrase that she abhorred. She thought

that Thornton Wilder's *Our Town* was false, and so was Heming-
way's prose pose of virility. She had no taste for Abstract Painting
and for Supermodern Architecture: but she saw through Andrew
Wyeth's "Americanist" realism: to her Wyeth was a cold-hearted
and cold-eyed illustrator, a calculated fit to the Eisenhower
decade. Do not think that she was severe or habitually critical.
She was not. She admired Stonewall Jackson and Charles de
Gaulle (she once said about the latter that he "made something
out of nothing"). She loved the voices of Al Jolson and Charles Az-
navour. These preferences of hers were not contradictory at all.

Her inclinations toward and her disinclinations to Catholicism were examples of her honesty. She knew nothing about the
Catholic Church, she had no Catholic acquaintances or friends
before she met me. Then the horizon of her knowledge of the
Church widened because of her acquaintance with many Catholics, often through my association with Catholic colleges, also
through her reading. Soon after our marriage she said that she
found much to admire in the realism of the Catholic teaching of
human nature, of its duality and moral range, including sinfulness, free will, grace. But more than once she was set aback by the
talk of some of the priests who visited us, by their efforts to impress people (and now her, their Protestant hostess) that they
were regular fellows, like all other Americans. H. never asked
much from people; but she had expected more from these American Catholic priests. Yet . . . five days before she died in the hospital, she asked for a priest and came into the Roman Catholic

Church. She is buried in the same small grave together with the ashes of my mother, of my aunt, and of my second wife, Stephanie. I stop and gaze at their small gravestones when I walk through the parish churchyard on some Sundays to Mass.

Somehow she understood that an entire civilization was unraveling and sinking, that Civilization was more important than Culture, and that this was no longer a philistine preference. (If indeed it ever had been.) I never remember her as girlish: she must have matured early in her life. These stumbling phrases of mine are my attempt to memorialize—more; to immortalize—her. "Exegi monumentum aere perennius"? A feeble but dutiful attempt. I have, perhaps unduly, stressed the quality of her mind. But so much more important is what remains engraved in my memory (and, I hope, in that of our son): her unfailing kindness, the instant red goodness of her heart. And that was American too.

Her death may have spared her more suffering, including a further darkening view of her country and its people. It did not spare her children, who were now bereft of an exceptional mother.

■

I was not bereft of a wife for long. Three and a half years later I married Stephanie.

To describe her is not easy. She had a beautiful figure, always sitting up straight, lovely legs, and a jewel-like face, piquant, with an inimitable smile, above which flickered her nervous, pale blue eyes and thin dark-blond hair, attractive beyond imagination.* She was, and remained, youthful through her entire life. She died in her seventy-seventh year. I have many photographs of her, including one when she was past seventy-one, sitting on a terrace in the California wine country, lifting high a glass of white wine, sparkling sunlight and sparkling Stephanie smile: a young fiftyish woman at most. Her beauty was very American. Alajálov was a Russian who painted many covers for the *New Yorker* in the late 1940s and early 1950s. Their favorite feature and figures were young American girls, pixyish blondes. Alajálov met S. when she was eighteen, working in the Western Union office in Palm Beach. He fell in love with her. She did not model for him, but she saw him in New York once or twice. That was the vagabond period of her life. (She loved the books of Colette; her favorite was *Le Vagabond*, about Colette's father. I once heard a French woman singer croon: "Je suis vagabonde mais fidèle." Fit S. to a T.)

I went to Europe for all kinds of reasons, including research, almost every year after H. died. Often my first stop was Milan, for Vera and Jancsi, this bourgeois couple from old Budapest, the

---

*D. 29 December 2000 (after more than a quarter-century of marriage). "The big plus in my life is S., *la trouvaille*. She has many faults, and has about given up washing & ironing my shirts. But, nearing 75, her flesh is still apricot and her spirit emerald."

D. 16 October 2001. "I tell S. how beautiful she looked Sunday, to which I add that she had of course little or no competition. She says that this annuls everything I just said."

once closest friends of my mother. All through my life in America I wanted to bring my old and my new worlds together. In 1972, in Venice: "Vera," I said. "I'm going to marry again." "Yes?" she said. "Does she have money?" "Not one red cent," I said. "Besides, she has four bad children." Vera gave me a queer look; then she buried her face in her hands. "Are you insane? What would your mother say?" I tried to laugh. "How right you are. But: This is the most beautiful woman in the world."

Reader: of course I married her. Two years later. Again our first stop was Milan, where Vera, chic and smart, took S. aside after a small champagne dinner in their airy apartment high above the streets and the tops of the trees in the gardens of rich Milanese. When we rode away to our hotel in a taxi, S. suddenly said: "Damn it! Did you see that Vera pulled me aside to talk to me? She said that I should understand that I am married to a European man. Damn it! I should have had the nerve to tell her that, yes, and he is married to an American woman."*

That was the one and only occasion of her esprit d'escalier, when her repartee was not split-second, instant. She had not a

---

*Twenty-two years later Vera and her husband were dead, and we made another quick stop in Milan to meet their daughter and Ila. S. said: "Let's try to avoid that, all those pecks on cheeks, kissies and kissies, with their perfumes and jeweled wrists." Somewhat later, in America at a party, someone about me: "He is *so* European." S.: "No, he is not *so* European." Somewhat later I to her: "There is no one like you." S.: "There is no one like you, either, but don't let that get into your head."

trace of French blood, she knew only a little French, but she was a Francophile, with a genuine love for French novels, poems, painting, and of course food. She was very Parisienne, in many ways: *vivace, spirituelle, fougueuse*. I am writing this because of her rare and superb combination of mind: her wit (almost French), her sense of humor (very English).* Was she self-educated? An autodidact? No, she was much more than that: a superb reader. She had not gone to college but to the Pennsylvania Academy of Fine Arts. Her knowledge of English literature larked high above that of many college or university professors of English. She knew and could cite Shakespearean lines at a trice. Who were some favorite writers of hers? Willa Cather and Jane Austen. Colette and Bernanos. Santayana and Saint Teresa of Avila. Trollope and Isak Dinesen. Saki and Edward Lear. Her most admired

---

*Examples. A woman: "John must be interesting; he understands women." S.: "What he does not know about women is certainly worth knowing." Whining speech of a famous New York woman writer: S.: "Interminable." Once in Hungary I was praised by Hungarians. S.: "Are you now one of their Wise Men? Some country this is." It is 1987, the centenary of the Statue of Liberty and Ellis Island; a woman, effusive, at a college reception turns to me: "You must tell us when and how *you* came to America." S.: "He came on the Concorde." Home from Vienna, I tell her that I met this excellent woman historian (Brigitte Hamann), who is a good-looking fifty-eight. S.: "You did not have to tell me *that*." One night, in my cups, from across the ocean I rang her up at home in Pennsylvania, telling her how I enjoyed talking to a lovely woman at an unexpected dinner party. S.: "Is that so? The furnace man was here this morning and called me 'darling.'"

painter was Pissarro. Her rapturous recording was Gluck's *Orfeo ed Euridice.* When I fell in love with her I hummed "I've Got a Crush on You" in her ear. She was charmed by the gesture but indifferent to that music. She was a supple, an embraceable dancer.

I once quoted to her Valéry Larbaud: "There are two kinds of faithfulness in love: one is finding ever new things in the loved one; the other is the pride of being faithful." "With you," I told her, "that is easy." A friend once described me as "a closet monogamist." True enough, we laughed, and were content.

There was one element in our relationship that was the opposite of mine with H. I think that I had more of an influence on S. than she would have on me. But that took some time. Our marriage had much trouble at the beginning. She had not had a peaceful childhood. She, too, was the offspring of parents unsuited to each other. Her mother was willful, sexy, partly of Pennsylvania-German blood. Her father, from the deepest South (Mississippi) was orphaned early, deeply honest, chivalrous and naïve. He was studying architecture at the University of Pennsylvania when he met and married S.'s mother. She was very young then. They moved to Palm Beach, where he designed and built noteworthy (and some still preserved) buildings. They had three daughters. S. was the youngest, born in 1926, the year when the Florida land boom collapsed suddenly, her father's money going down with it in toto. His quondam prosperity never recovered. Nor did his marriage. His wife chose to run a restaurant of her own; then she decided to go to Europe for a year, taking her five-year-old daughter with her; she divorced her husband and married a quiet Englishman, a fine painter who killed himself in 1945, when S. was nineteen.*

From this, very American-Floridian climate of relentless sun, beaches, cottages, parties, of moneyless living, of many easy commas and a few hard question marks, S. went to Philadelphia to study painting. In the bucolic setting of the summer school of the Academy in Chester Springs, she met her husband, handsome, a very good painter, a few months younger than she. They married when she was twenty-two. Then they had four children, born every two years. They had very little money. He struggled, admirably, to provide for her and for the children. They led an existence that was bohemian, but there was nothing louche in their lives, not at all like the Palm Beach climate. They had a small circle of friends in what was then still very rural Chester County. Then came the 1960s, and that took a toll (if that is the right word) on their children, teenagers during that sordid (yes, sordid) decade. They were undisciplined; and often troublesome. That was first an unspoken obstacle to, and then a source of considerable troubles for, our marriage. My two children were better off than were hers. They went to private schools and to colleges. They had their own cars: hers could and did not. The fact—and

---

*Many years later her mother and father remarried. It was not a good remarriage, and it did not last long. S.'s mother, with her erstwhile charms ravaged, stumbled to her death at seventy. Her father, about whom anon, survived her by more than a quarter-century, lived to be ninety-seven.

it was a very good fact, rare in cases of children of different marriages—that my two children liked their stepbrothers and stepsister was not enough to assuage her unhappiness with our marriage. Nor was it enough to eliminate my unhappiness with the behavior of some of my new stepchildren, living with us now. Even that was not all. S. had now inherited my orphaned daughter, five years old, protected and cosseted before that by her father and by Peggy, my Irish housekeeper, who doted on Annemarie but who had to leave when I married S., who was not a good stepmother.* Not a bad one, but at times indifferent. And so Annemarie and I lived through years of heartaches of our own. And much of this was part of something that I had not really thought of before: that now not only her children but S. herself had to accommodate herself to a bourgeois, yes, bourgeois existence, to standards, values, aspirations, and conditions that, even if comfortable and secure, were different from what she had been used to in the past. There was a moment—more precisely, two months—when our marriage nearly broke up.

And then one or two years went by, and some of our troubles went away. She became accustomed to my ideas of a bourgeois existence. That involved more than an acceptance of security and comfort. (Throughout her life she was indifferent to money, al-

---

*D. 28 October 2006. "I read a story by Defoe where I find that in 17th-cent. English (and probably later too) 'mother-in law' was used for stepmother. (Logically / legally this makes sense.)"

most to the point of ignorance.) I think I taught her that *bourgeois* (a word that I am using here merely for purposes of intellectual shorthand) did not mean philistinism, not at all. On one of our journeys, in Stockholm, we were in the beautiful, airy, seaside house of Mme Ytte Bonnier, furnished and breathing with a fresh autumnal climate of high taste and great intelligence. I told S.: "This atmosphere, this house, these people are not aristocrats; this is high bourgeois and this is what is now the very best in the world." Now she understood this. But then her very choices, her tastes had changed. Social ambitions she did not have. But she felt at ease not only with my intellectual and academic but with my Chester County old-American friends, who, in turn, fast accepted her as one of theirs. She had never been interested in politics, but that changed, by a little, too: it was she, not I, who came to read the *New York Times* every morning; and her comments and judgments sometimes made me say that she was becoming a connoisseuse of politics, a new (my) Lady Holland. Her once latent but instinctive American patriotism became more and more conscious. She was appalled by what mass immigration from Central America was doing to her native places in Florida. She also found herself repelled by the loud prominence of New York Intellectuals. She said that what they knew was very little, ephemeral, and largely worthless: a smidgeon of city-America, if even that.

And so, perhaps less than a decade after our wedding, our marriage became a near-idyll. It was further annealed by her old father, who had come to live with us for the last four years of his life, and whom I loved. We built a house together. S. and I were still very different in temperament: I got up early in the morning, she late; I went to bed early, she late; she never made me breakfast or lunch; but how often, night after night, we sat at the dinner table (she was a delicious cook) for one, sometimes even two hours, talking about many things under the sun and the moon. She was a wonderfully acute critic of my books as I wrote them.* My children and her children had come closer to each of us. I thought that she would survive me: but the opposite came. In *Confessions* I wrote a page or so about the death of H. Now I must of S.

Procrastination was a fault of hers. She should have had her hips replaced many years before she accepted to have that done. She was not yet seventy when, going through a museum, I had to move her in a wheelchair. But she was still desirable, so beautiful, so desirable. In the seventy-seventh summer of her life, she became gradually more and more tired and also depressed. I struggled with her to come with me to our doctor. She said no, and then she agreed, but on the day before that planned visit, she suddenly became very weak and ill. I and her daughter Hilary took her to the local emergency ward. Her blood pressure was

---

*I dedicated at least two of my books to her; but the last sentence of my Acknowledgments in one of them (*Five Days in London*) tells all. "My wife, Stephanie, reads everything—well, almost everything—that I write; her comments are often funny and incisive, reflections of her sparkling and charming personality, a benison for a manuscript as it is for a man's life."

down, but all tests were negative. An impulse made me ask the doctor to have one more test done, a CAT scan of her head. Ah! There was a tumor in her brain. She had to be operated on instantly. So she was, three days later. Having carved out the tumor, the surgeon told us that she might have no more than a year, perhaps a year and a half, to live.*

She died five months later. Need I say that I tried everything; contacts and consultations with the very best experts I could raise, but of course in vain? Need I describe the awful dilemma that I had experienced before with H. and now with S.? It is a dilemma that some of my readers may recognize, the dilemma of the last days (or weeks) of a loved one. Do we wish that she live a little longer, or do we wish that she die sooner rather than later? And why? To relieve *her* of further suffering; or to relieve—selfishly—*ourselves?* Do we—can we—honestly know?† Let me record something else, instead: that there were consolations. My

---

*D. 13 August 2002. "I will now lose my darling, I, who said (and hoped) that one day she would be a Merry Widow."

†All I can say in my behalf is that my agony could not have been entirely selfish: I wrote in my diary that I would have gladly exchanged my life for hers in a moment.

D. 7 February 2005. "There is no such thing as *pure* unselfishness. (Perhaps some saints (not all of them) have come close to it but not entirely, i.e., "purely." But there is no such thing as pure selfishness either (since that almost always has some element of despair): yet so many people can come close, v. close to achieving it."

diary of 23 November 2002, Saturday, after which I stopped writing it for long months: "Today we brought her home from the hospital, to die. Yet this was a day of some brightness and sweetness." Probably because I knew that now she would remain at home, in our bedroom, in her bed, from that very day to her very last. And so it was, surrounded by all who loved her, foremost by her youngest son, Charles, who had dropped everything to come to live with us, nursing and caring for her with such extraordinary dedication; but by her other children too; and by my son and his wife, who came up from Baltimore almost every week; and by my daughter, who came every second day; and by friends; and once by her former husband; and then one somber afternoon our friend Father Meehan came to visit her. I had been downstairs: but then I learned that she had asked for Confession and Communion and Last Rites. (Much later Father Meehan said that she said the "Domine non sum dignus" in Latin.) She, who except for a short flirtation with Roman Catholicism in the early 1960s (before the new Mass and Vatican II) had declared herself Episcopalian, now came back (back?) into the Church too.* That night she said to me: "You don't know what Father

*D. 6 October 2002. "I went to Mass, with a dry soul & mind. After the priest started his sermon with a joke (as customary with him) he assured the parishioners that they'll be home in plenty of time for the Eagles' game. I stood up and walked out. Didn't do this to be demonstrative. But walked out w. a sense of relief, even more than of indignation. I knew then and I know now that this was wrong. I had come to pray for Stephanie and I hardly did so."

Meehan's coming meant to me." By Christmas she could hardly speak. On New Year's morning I: "Good morning, darling." She muttered something. Four days later, on Sunday, the nurse called me from the room where I was getting awake. Her bed was surrounded by Charles and two nurses. I had the privilege to lean over her now sad little face in the moment she died.* "I will be with you forever,"† I babbled, full of tears. There then came the fret and fuss of the necessities. And then the saddest moment. I had gone upstairs to her at noon. She was already growing cold. Then the funeral directors came. She was taken away from this house, forever. I watched the car moving down our driveway and then gathering speed. It had begun to snow.

Four days later more than two hundred people came to her funeral at Saint Mary's, and then to our house. How did some of them know? I had put an obituary only in the local paper. In it I put, *anglice:* "The benevolence of her heart, the sweetness of her temperament, the extraordinary endowments of her mind, ob-

---

*Both Helen and Stephanie died on a Sunday morning, exactly at half past seven, thirty-three years apart. Both turned Catholic before their death. Both rest in the same grave.

†D. 25 July 2006. "I know (but how?) that there is a world after this; and that nothing of our nature will replicate or exist there. But here is my worry: that *memory* will not there exist. If so, how can we hope to see our loved ones again, if at all? Memory is not just one factor in our brain, not just one element of our consciousness. It is involved with *all* of it. (Hence, too, the importance of history as the fundamental element of human knowledge.)"

tained the regard of all who knew her and the warmest love of her intimate family. (As on Jane Austen's tombstone in Winchester Cathedral.)" In our living room I said a last toast to her and, *more hungarico*, smashed a glass charged with her lately favorite wine* against the fireplace.[†]

From a woman, a friend who had grown distant from us in later years, a memorable letter which is framed on the back of S.'s photograph on my desk: "What can I say except to commend you for your choice of an exceptional woman. You and Stephanie truly were made for each other, something that happens rarely, as you know. You were a match in every sense of the word." Our English friend Michael (M. R. D.) Foot wrote: "Stephanie always seemed to me to have something evanescent about her, as if a strong gale of wind might carry her clear away—alas. Such a splendid instance of American womanhood . . . " Yes, that she was.

Yes, *pace* Valéry Larbaud: I found ever more and more things to love in her, till the very end. And beyond that too: one enduring blessing. Her children and I, especially Charles, but not only

---

*An Alboriño. Helen's was a Valpolicella.

[†]And then, to my stunned American friends I spoke my slight variant of Scott's dirge:

> Now is the stately column broke
> The beacon-light is quench'd in smoke
> The silver of her voice is still
> Her warder silent on the hill.

Charles, have come closer and closer. (Her former husband too, now embraces me whenever we occasionally meet.) *Fata trahunt . . .*

■

I have learned something about myself that I may not have consciously recognized in the past, which is my, perhaps extraordinary, need for a woman. This must be a romantic weakness of which sexual desire is but one, and seldom the dominant part—certainly not now but not even in my youth (or so I think). A woman? More than that: a woman, at home for me and with me. A quest for such arose soon, so very soon, after S.'s death. I did not think that I was unfaithful or disloyal to her: she would have understood. My excuse is simple: I was vulnerable. Yet wounds and gouges and cicatrices are external, they maim and afflict a body from the outside. I afflicted myself; my wounds were self-made.

Less than six months after S.'s death I was introduced to a woman in Hungary who attracted me at once. She was full-blooded, almost Junoesque, with a natural aura of deep brown earthiness, with a strong mind and a vibrant and erotic spirit, an expressive Hungarian face capable of sardonic smiles, a strong hard body in a few cheap but not shabby second-hand pieces of clothing. She was willing to be introduced to me by my friend Alex. She knew nothing about me. She found me older than expected, which I certainly was. I went to work on her fast. She was about to leave Budapest for her place in the country. The morning after we met I telephoned her and asked her to come to my palatial suite. It was a Sunday, the staff was gone, I coursed down the street to get some cakes; she came in summery rags, bringing me fresh raspberries and more. Instantly I invited her to come visit me in America. She said yes. She pecked a kiss on my cheek as I dropped her at her apartment house in a taxi.

I fell in love with her very soon. She sent me a recent photograph of her: hair dripping with damp, her countenance crimson colored and wide-mouthed, large eyes, high summer in a boat on a Hungarian river. I could not keep my eyes from that picture the moment it arrived. I called her every few days, then every day from across the Atlantic. Wrote her long letters. I had fallen?— no, I made myself fall in love with her. I sent her an enormous bouquet of flowers on her birthday, and a wad of money for her airfare and then some. I counted the days, the hours, the minutes before she would land in Philadelphia on the first day of October. When she strode with her strong legs out of the International Arrivals corridor, I was lifted by a huge wave of happiness.

She spent three weeks with me here in my Pennsylvania house and then, three months later, I flew to spend a month with her in her Budapest apartment. My passion for her was such that I came very close to marrying her. In the end, I stepped back from what would have been an abyss. She and I were incompatible. I can think only of two matters that may be of any interest to my readers. One is my experience and conviction that physical passion is still possible for a seventy-nine- or eighty-year-old man.* And why? because of the powers of imagination. Twenty-one years separated us; her earthly sexuality was much younger and stronger than mine, but this mattered not much. What mattered was the incompatibility of our minds, of our temperaments, of our history. The past, my past? To go *back* to Hungary, to live in a dark house, in an apartment full of shadows, with her? and there to die? There *was* such a subterranean pull: but I was conscious enough to resist it. One element of her Hungarianness that would have been disastrous in a marriage, and that had already produced black little disasters during our living together, was her volcanic temperament: alas, uncontrolled and selfish. The other was her history—or, rather, her view of history. Forty years of life under Communism did not make her a Communist or anything like that: rather the contrary. The fact that she had been married and divorced and had had a number of lovers did not deter me: the trouble was not with her past but with her aspirations. She had a tremendous appetite for anything that was "new": in art, poetry, music, dancing, clothing, manners, and morals, men and women living beyond respectable limits. She adored New York (she had

*(Conversely): D. 19 December 2000. "When an older woman is made love to, her happiness is a compound of emotions such as duty, gratitude, vanity, pleasure. These are matters that Freud, etc., did not, or perhaps could not deal with. They are not simple: for example, there is a flowing of duty and gratitude into each other; vanity is not quite the same thing as self-esteem."

been there before, once); she wanted to go to New Orleans, preferably for its rowdy Mardi Gras. (From what I saw of her family she was an admirable mother and grandmother: but then such is the alchemy of human, perhaps especially of women's nature.)

I had to break away from her. That was not easy. I kept her photograph on my desk for another two months or so.*

■

A little more than a year later I married Pamela, my third American wife, whom I met accidentally, without any plan, and whom then I came to love and love more and more. Again it was I, not she, who wanted marriage. Her presence in my life became indispensable—and for more than practical reasons. I will not, perhaps I cannot, imagine my remaining years without her. She is twenty-three years younger than I, energetic, with lovely eyes and a beautiful profile. She was a divorcée when I met her, struggling through difficult years after a long and childless and eventually unhappy marriage. After her marriage had been annulled, we were married by Father Meehan. She always wanted children. Now she has my two children and my four stepchildren, of whom at least two are close to us. My daughter is very close to her.

On a short honeymoon we drove to the Greenbrier, a famous, big, rich, resort hotel on the edge of her native state, West Virginia. The Greenbrier was an icon in her memory; her parents

*D. 5 August 2005. "Few things are sadder than forgotten friendships. (*Not* so with forgotten loves.)"

had stopped there on occasion. I found it appalling. It had all of
the symptoms and symbols, signs and sounds and presences of
an, alas, so very Republican-American party riches and standards
and customs and vanities. Enormous halls, enormous dining
rooms, enormous golf courses, enormous greenswards, marbled
corridors with glitzy shops, walls with many framed photos and
letters from Dwight Eisenhower, Spiro Agnew, Dick Nixon,
Ronald Reagan, most of them addressed to Sam Snead, a golfer for
whom shrines and highways and courses are named. Men and
women pace across them, the men chortling with false cama-
raderie, the women dressed up and devoid of chic. They are the
new new rich, "upscale," a recent stupid adjective they hope is
affixable to them. Affixed, too, to most of their big, shiny automobiles are vanity plates. When on a rainy afternoon we walked
into the large and rich Outfitters' Shop, I knew that I did not belong here, not in the least. I was not an American sportsman but
a fortuneless immigrant who had not and could not dare have
anything in common with the providers and riflers of this fabu-
lous amount and variety of goods, with these ranks of Sam's and
Dick's and Ron's people. I was a foreigner, alien and uninvited, as
out of place and out of time* as at a Nascar race or the Super Bowl.

*One additional and truly damning fact about the Greenbrier. Underneath
its big pile, in 1959 the government began to construct a monstrous under-
ground city to which half a thousand appointed and elected persons would repair, transported thereto in case of a nuclear war. This was revealed by the
Washington Post after the end of the cold war, in 1992, I think. It is now empty,

The next morning we drove on long roads along the silent un-peopled gray and green hills of West Virginia to Pamela's native city, Charleston, to the house where she was born and where she spent her childhood and early youth, 1633 Quarrier Street. Her parents had died. Their modest house was empty. It was kept up by her sister, and Pamela had the keys. We could stay there for a night or two. There was the always ancient dusty and musty smell of an empty house, empty even with its heavy mahogany beds and other oaken furniture. Empty of books it was not. Her father's den full of old law books, the bookcases on the wall of their living room or parlor lined with biographies and novels and histories of the America of the 1930s and 1940s, of a decent, hon-est, still book-reading, middle class. Nothing in this house was plastic. It was something of a silent museum, in its silence a piece of the world of Harry Truman. So this was where my now third American wife was born, and where her father and mother had brought her up. We went to her parents' grave, to the cemetery up on a hill, a stone's throw away from a memorial where Union and Confederate soldiers were buried together. I was moved. I knew that I had married well again.

---

shown to the Greenbrier's guests on occasion, if and when they wish to see it. I find it both telling and damning that the Eisenhower administration chose to begin building it in 1959, when the worst years of the cold war were over, in the very year when Nikita Khrushchev was begging to be invited to come to Wash-ington and to visit Disneyland. (He was allowed the first but not the second.)

Now I sit often on our terrace, surrounded by Pamela's constantly evolving declarations of flowers. Now we have suburban neighbors, in their large houses on the former fields of what was for 250 years the farm of my first wife's ancestors: but there is enough wild shrubbery and trees between us that we do not see them, except when the leaves and branches have fallen, in the winter. My green backyard slopes down to the water. There is much work to be done on house, field, terrace garden, and the great sheet of water before us is silting up, and I cannot do anything about that. But my third American wife helps and will help me. Where I sit and breathe is still my, now our, achievement, my Arcadia, our modest paradise. Pourvu que cela dure.*

■

We have our shortcomings, and I fear that mine will grow worse with age, each year, perhaps even each month. She knows my dualities, and I know hers. She differs from me. She has little respect for my pessimism. She is American, after all. I have not yet convinced her that it is so much easier to be unhappy than to be happy. But she is coming around to agree that happiness is a task.

Do women want to be happy? That is too vague. What they want is to have a reason for being happy.

I am, of course, deeply aware that when a civilization crumbles,

---

*"If it will only last": the famous words of Napoleon's Corsican mother when messenger after messenger brought her news of the triumphs of her son.

that involves the very relations of the sexes. Equality is not, it must not be, uniformity. The other day I read an obiter dictum, something that Tocqueville wrote, more than 170 years ago. "It is easy to see that in thus striving to equal the sexes one degrades them both; and that nothing could ever come of such a gross confusion of Nature's work but weak men and unchaste women." Perhaps not nothing: but not much. After all, love *has* become rarer, alas. More than fifty years ago in *The End of the Modern World*, Romano Guardini wrote: "Love will disappear from the face of the public* world (Matthew 24:12), but the more precious will that love be which flows from one lonely person to another, involving a courage of the heart born from the immediacy of the love of God. . . . Perhaps man will come to experience this love anew, to sense the mystery of its final why? Perhaps love will achieve an intimacy and harmony never known to this day." Yes, that "perhaps" is possible, says I, this Hungarian pessimist, this Original Sinner. When we love someone we see her as God sees her—I said that, more than once, to my wives. That has always been true. But in America I have learned something else too, which is that love is *practical.* Do not say *that* to your American wife. She might say: "Yes. Now please go and empty the dishwasher."

---

*But not from the false and obscene grinning presentation of its publicity.

SEVEN

Ave atque Vale

More than twenty years ago I wrote (and repeated this once in this book too): that I have had a happy unhappy life, which is preferable to an unhappy happy one. I even thought to terminate this book with this same phrase, ending it with: *stet*. But now, in the eighty-fifth year of my life, this phrase does not quite ring so true. Perhaps now it is the other way around. I do not know. Twenty years ago I was still traveling "dans les faubourgs de la viellesse," ambling in the suburbs of old age. The gates and walls of that stony city I saw at a distance. No longer.

There is another, perhaps unduly self-confident phrase, one with verve and panache, that I used to dress my mind (and flesh) and wear it, almost publicly: that my (masculine?) desire to please is stronger than (and prior to) my wish to be loved. This too, I confess, may no longer be so. My desire to please is not yet extinct: but how much I want and need the love of my third wife, of my children, of my friends!

I write still. Thackeray in *Henry Esmond:* "As there are a thousand thoughts lying within a man that he does not know till he takes up the pen to write." Very true for compulsive writers (though probably not for e-mail users). Often writing clarifies, and even enriches, a writer's mind—yet another example of how the functions of the human mind do not follow the "laws" of matter. The contradiction of this duality: both richer and lighter—is not measurable.

Ave before *Vale.* Looking backward: how many dualities were, and still are, in my mind, indeed, in my character! To list them, to describe them, do not belong in this book, which is not a confession. But I think I owe confession of one duality, addressed to my historically minded readers: a duality, indeed, a contradiction (in the literal meaning of that latter word). I am, I was, a man in the short twentieth century, a remnant reactionary, a remnant self-proclaimed bourgeois, a remnant admirer of the civilization and the culture of the past five hundred years, European and Western. Yet at the same time, and in the same mind— consider only the first thirty pages of this book!—I have recognized and realized and declared and written about how many of the dominant, ruling ideas and achievements of the past five hundred years were (or have become) wrong, antiquated, false: the ideas of Progress, of Objectivity, of Evolution, of Materialism, of Uniform Equality, of Geometrical and Mathematical

Truth, of the Enlightenment, indeed, of the Universe, etc., etc. About this duality of mine I think I owe something of a brief explanation or, rather, an excuse. Those, eventually governing and ruling, ideas of the Bourgeois Age (that, and not "the Modern Age," is the proper designation of the past five hundred years) were not and are not entirely wrong: what was, and is still, wrong is their institutionalization, the acceptance of their formulation as absolutes.

As indeed the substitution of Reason for Faith. Yes, there is reason to lament that our churches have been emptying, that there are fewer faithful believers, something that is ascertainable from their acts or from the absence of their acts. But at the same time—by which I mean: at *this* time—there are evidences (not decisive ones, perhaps not even important ones, at best, a few significant ones, but no matter) that the Christian beliefs of the original sinfulness of men, of their free will, perhaps even of the immortality of the human soul, have somehow seeped into the minds, lodging within the consciousnesses of hundreds of millions of nonchurchgoers, of nonbelievers, with traces that are not disappearing, not at all.

Let me now take a step down, not up: to a more concrete and tangible argument. This is that for most people in Europe and in America* there is an evident, and probably very telling differ-

---

*My thoughts and writings are directed to them. They are the people and the civilizations that I know. I must not and cannot make general statements about other peoples of the globe of whom I know regrettably very little, surely not enough.

ence between us and our ancestors of five hundred years ago. At that time brilliant people, thinkers, and artists, superb craftsmen, started to react against the age then just passed or passing: they turned away from many of its ideas and even achievements, the most learned among them looked back over what (later) came to be called the Middle Ages, they sought their inspiration from a, largely pagan, Rome and Greece, whence the words *rebirth*, *renaissance*. This is not what is happening now. We (yes, we, and not merely I) look back with admiration at the achievements and the art of the past five hundred years—we are not vaulting back over it to an idealized age before it. The achievements, including the art, of the past five hundred years will be more and more respected, they will continue to inspire all kinds of people, even if a small minority, in the twenty-first century and beyond. And this is something new: probably the result of the spreading of historical thinking—a principal result of the five hundred years behind us, the Bourgeois Age.

One last remark. The bourgeois: their hypocrisies, their materialism, their shallowness, the mental wasteland of the hollow men—all true, but altogether not true enough. Whence the hollowness in someone like Henry James's longing for a fading patriciandom with aristocratic tastes? There are glimpses of a very different longing in the writings of minor writers such as George Gissing and George Orwell, in one or two of their least known books. Both Gissing and Orwell excoriated the bourgeois and their world, with all of their destructive materialism, opportunism, selfishness. Yet in Gissing's *The Whirlpool* or in Orwell's *Keep the Aspidistra Flying* (neither of them their best books) despairing rebels find a small but definite measure of salvation in stepping down (rather than sinking) into the peace and tobacco-brown quietude of a modest bourgeois existence with their wives, conscious that even conforming to a few hypocrisies is preferable to intellectual dishonesty, the lees of a prevailing marriage better than the sour droplets of raging passions, and the shares of domesticity to the loneliness of illusory individualisms. Something else than defeat and resignation: a turning inward.

Winter evenings. I do not think that the Romans cherished them; nor did Elizabethans. I do. A month ago, on 16 February 2008 in my diary I wrote: " . . . I wasted almost three hours reading the *New York Times*, the *New York Review of Books*, and the London *Literary Review*. Then went for a half-hour walk in the cold. Then brought in wood and built a fire in the living room. Evening had come. I wondered: why this sudden fullness of mind and heart? Sitting there, looking at the flames in the fireplace? Because: this room, these few fine pieces of furniture in it, the dark amber and green and gold glow on the edges of some of them, the silence of the deep-red rug, the very existence of these things breathing here, extant from an older world, around me now, some things that I have rescued, bought, brought together, still here, still. Because of their value? No: because of their atmosphere."

Vale. Still my house; but not my "real estate." Not even my (our) garden. All "real estate" is ephemeral now, no longer very "real." But now a last peer into the future which, rather fortunately than not, remains unpredictable. I am a historian, still. I do not know what will happen; except that I know some things that will not happen. The barbarians are now well within the—largely demolished—gates. But what happens will again depend on what people think happens. That will not change. *How* people think may change: but that, too, not much, except perhaps for a further shrinking of their attention span. Already it seems that "Information Technology," computers, the Internet, blogs and e-mail did not and do not change much in the development of ideas and in their consequences.

Contrary to accepted ideas: the fear of "progress," of the future will grow, and so will respect for the past. My readers: please turn toward the past, and dip into its records and remnants, for inspiration. By doing that you may turn melancholy: but you will not lose your appetite for life. Quite the contrary. Such is yet another proof of the mystery of the human mind, indeed, of our earthly existence.

I regret that I am old. I regret that I fear the future and, yes, I fear a sudden death. I regret that my appetite for life has been weakening. I regret that so has my curiosity, my reading, and, together with that, perhaps even my very appetite for the past. But not weakening is my gratitude for the past. Ambition and greed invoke, they reach out to a future. Envy and pleasure insist on the present. But gratitude: it comes always from a past. There is my gratitude to the past, to my past, including those who loved me and whom I loved. Beneath and above them is my enduring gratitude to God, for both my past *and* my present. Will the sincerity of this gratitude suffice to escape His adverse judgment of me? I do not think so; I only hope.

◾

One, very last, remark—now not about my life but about those Bad Fifteen Minutes. My conviction of the grand truth that I cited and repeated innumerable times in my past writing and teaching, latent within a profound Portuguese proverb: "God writes straight with crooked lines." Everything made some sense—yes, everything. Sometime we may even glimpse that. "Clamat enim quodammodo omnis historia, Deus esse." "In a way all history cries aloud that God is" (Pope Leo XIII, who, among other things, ordered the opening of the Vatican archives). I read this after I finished this book.*

*In a review of a modest French symposium about Leo XIII (*Catholic Historical Review*, January 2008, page 161) by Owen Chadwick, *magister historiae!*